Praise for *The Stone Rejected by the Builders*

The Stone Rejected by the Builders: Some Uncommon Reflections on Social Justice, written by Reverend Joseph Levine and published by Arouca Press, is marked by uncommon wisdom, and represents everything I as a bishop would pray that a parish priest could be for his people and all whose lives he may touch.

Father Levine is getting out the essential message of Catholicism as it impacts not only those in the consecrated life, but especially as it seeks to enlighten the lives of the families, the men, women, and children in the pews. I suppose it is fair enough that he calls his reflections on Social Justice "uncommon", but only in the sense that true wisdom, the pearl of great price is indeed a rarity.

Father has an easy and readable style which opens up some pretty profound topics to one and all, regardless of their intellectual preparation. Some of my favorite parts are those dealing with marriage and family. The book is about as up to date as it can be.

My personal hope would be that priests especially, but also regular Catholics, would find ways to dive into this little book and acquaint themselves with what some might consider this uncommon worldview. For me, it might better be called extraordinary as "uncommon" sells it short. May many people take heart from Father's insights and find in them the courage to live the Gospel in light!

—✠**THE MOST REVEREND THOMAS E. GULLICKSON**, Tit. Archbishop of Bomarzo—Apostolic Nuncio

In this very insightful book Father Levine deals with the reality of the neo-pagan ideology that presently prevails in the United States—but more generally throughout the western world—in terms of "social justice" as understood in Catholic magisterial and foundational dogmatic and moral principles. He is a master of logic and unapologetic about the Catholic positions which he presents with clarity and espouses. At the same time, he recognizes that there is no simple way to turn things around in our topsy-turvy, godless world except by totally embracing and living Catholic life and liturgy as exemplified in the Blessed Virgin Mary for, as the Fathers of the Second Vatican Council put it: "Mary in a way unites in her person and re-echoes the most important doctrines of the faith" (*Lumen Gentium* #65).

—**REV. MSGR. ARTHUR B. CALKINS**

The term 'social justice' is often used— or abused— to support various ideological crusades. But what *is* social justice, and on what it is based? In this unusual book, Father Levine makes the perhaps startling argument that "the proper Sunday observance is at the foundation of true social justice."

To say that social justice starts with Sunday Mass is to take a radical stand. But for Catholics, for whom the Eucharistic liturgy is the "source and summit" of their faith, it makes sense. And in the course of the book, the author shows how a secularized understanding of the term not only fails to make sense, but leads to serious offenses against reason and human dignity.

—PHILIP LAWLER, author, Director of Catholic Culture & Editor of CWN

In clear, everyday language, Fr. Levine guides us through the current maze of relativism, through the story of creation, to a sure understanding of the principles underlying the Church's teaching on social justice. Along the way, he offers startling insights on the importance of the family, work, the role of the state, and the common good, all ordered to the life of grace here and glory hereafter. A brilliant and engrossing presentation of the Church's perennial social teaching.

—SAMUEL A. SCHMITT, MLM, PhD, Director of Sacred Music and Organist, Sts. Cyril and Methodius Church

In his magnificent work, *The Stone Rejected by the Builders*, Fr. Levine sets forth both the philosophical and theological foundations of Social Justice. Emanating not only from his many years of experience as a pastor of souls, but also from his profound wisdom and love for Holy Scripture, as well as a breathtaking knowledge of the Church doctors and fathers, *The Stone Rejected by the Builders* is as compelling as it is lucid. It is brief and eminently readable. Comprehensive in its scope, every reader will gain an understanding of the fundamental principles of social justice, while also realizing that the denial of these principles account for nearly all of the disorders in our world. In particular, readers will be stunned by the demonstration that the Holy Sacrifice of the Mass is central to Social Justice. Written for the layman, Fr. Levine has managed to present "uncommon reflections" which will also be enormously beneficial to the academic. This potentially life changing book belongs on the shelves of every Chancery, Seminary, Secondary school, College and University and, indeed, on the shelves of every Catholic.

—MARK LANGLEY, Founder, The Lyceum, South Euclid, Ohio; Headmaster, Our Lady of Walsingham Academy, Colorado Springs, Colorado

THE STONE REJECTED
BY THE BUILDERS

THE STONE
REJECTED BY
THE BUILDERS

SOME UNCOMMON
REFLECTIONS ON
SOCIAL JUSTICE

JOSEPH LEVINE

AROUCA
PRESS

ISBN: 978-1-990685-70-5 (pbk)
ISBN: 978-1-990685-71-2 (hc)

Arouca Press
PO Box 55003
Bridgeport PO
Waterloo, ON N2J 0A5
Canada
www.aroucapress.com
Send inquiries to info@aroucapress.com

Cover design by
Julian Kwasniewski
Cover image: window in
the Caleruega Friars' Chapel,
courtesy of Fr Lawrence Lew, OP

CONTENTS

"Hear another parable. There was a householder who planted a vineyard, and set a hedge around it, and dug a wine press in it, and built a tower, and let it out to tenants, and went into another country. When the season of fruit drew near, he sent his servants to the tenants, to get his fruit; and the tenants took his servants and beat one, killed another, and stoned another. Again he sent other servants, more than the first; and they did the same to them. Afterward he sent his son to them, saying, 'They will respect my son.' But when the servants saw the son, they said to themselves, 'This is the heir; come, let us kill him and have his inheritance.' And they took him and cast him out of the vineyard, and killed him. When therefore the owner of the vineyard comes, what will he do to those tenants?" They said to him, "He will put those wretches to miserable death, and let out the vineyard to other tenants who will give him the fruits in their seasons." Jesus said to them, "Have you never read in the scriptures: '*The very stone which the builders rejected has become the head of the corner*; this was the Lord's doing and it is marvelous in our eyes'? Therefore I tell you, the kingdom of God will be taken away from you and given to a nation producing fruits of it. And he who falls on this stone will be broken to pieces; but when it falls on anyone, it will crush him." (Matt. 21:33–44)

DEDICATION

In honor of Our Lady of Fatima,
Without whom I would have never
been ordained to the priesthood.
May her Immaculate Heart triumph,
Bringing in the reign of Christ the King.
May he reign over hearts, over
families, over nations.

ACKNOWLEDGEMENTS

OVER THE YEARS MANY PEOPLE HAVE urged me to publish, usually my homilies, because that is what they had heard or read. Fr. Gary Selin, who has read various of my essays and musings, has from time to time encouraged me to seek publication for one or another of them. So, in the first place, I want to thank all those who have encouraged me, even if this first book is not what they had in mind.

In preparing this work for publication, I sent a draft to various friends. Mark Langley was thrilled to get a copy and when all was said and done made some small contributions to the clarity of the text. His brother Michael read it and expressed his enthusiasm. Thank you to both of you for your friendship and support over many years. Thank you to Christy Wall for your suggestions for the Introduction. A special thanks to Jensiy Bryan for carefully reading, commenting, and proofreading the whole work.

I must also thank those whom I served in the parish of St. Peter's in The Dalles, for whom I originally wrote the collection of essays that was the origin of this book. You taught me so much about what it means to be a priest.

I also want to express my gratitude for Thomas Aquinas College because without the education I received there I would never have been able to write this book. So also to the founding president, Dr. Ronald McArthur, a true giant of a man, whom I was privileged to call a friend, may he rest in peace.

Finally, a word about the publisher, Arouca Press, I discovered what wonderful work they are doing. The first time I ordered any books from Arouca Press, I received a prompt personal note from the founder. What service. And what fine works, new and old, they are putting into print, with such great enthusiasm! I have met with the same enthusiasm, welcome, and encouragement since I first submitted *The Stone Rejected* to the publisher. It has been a pleasure.

INTRODUCTION

I BEGAN THIS SERIES OF ESSAYS IN 2019, when I was pastor of St. Peter Catholic Church in The Dalles, Oregon. I had been pastor there for almost seven years; we had just finished another "catechetical year" and were heading into the summer, when many people decide to take a vacation from Mass. In the Pacific Northwest, one of our rival "religions" is "the great out-doors," so I thought it might be good, while the beauty of God's creation was in the forefront of many people's mind, even if the Creator was not, to write a series of essays for the parish bulletin on the theme of 'creation.' This also required writing something about the relation between science and faith. As was often the case, when I started a series of essays for the parish bulletin, it took me more than the few weeks originally planned.

In this case, the treatment of "creation" which con-cluded with some reflections on the account of the seven days in Genesis, did not take too long and I was done by the end of October. Nevertheless, my reflections on the seventh day led me to ponder how the worship of God is truly the cornerstone of human social life and so therefore the cornerstone of "social justice"; likewise, *male and female he created them*, which reveals husband and wife as the primeval human society, led me to consider the centrality of marriage in human social life and therefore any true "social justice."

So, I had found the theme for my next series of essays, "Social Justice." This series took me from November 2019 all the way until April 2021. After I began writing we experienced the Covid lockdown, the BLM riots (when I first heard that acronym I was puzzled because in these parts BLM means "Bureau of Land Management") which were particularly prominent and prolonged just down the interstate in Portland, and a rather controversial

Presidential election, capped by the events of January 6, 2021.

My goal as a parish priest is quite simple really: to lead men to faith, from faith to holiness, from holiness to eternal salvation. That means bringing them from wherever they are in their day-to-day life into a deepening relation with Jesus Christ, Son of God and Mediator between God and men. Alas, social injustice impacts them in countless ways in their day-to-day life.

We can start with the 24/7 rhythm of contemporary secular life. It seems that most people live in a world in which time is divided between "the work week" and "the weekend," which is for recreation or catching up on chores and maybe "church" as an optional add-on. Yet, that same 24/7 work week also requires many people, who might otherwise want to attend Mass, to work on Sundays. This was certainly the case in a parish with a large Mexican immigrant population.[1]

Next, I could consider the social injustice of the public school system, mandatory for those who cannot afford another option. Such was the case for the majority of my parishioners who could not afford to send their children to our parish school and were incapable of homeschooling their children because both parents needed to work outside the home—another social injustice—and because the parents themselves did not speak English and had often not even attended high school.

---

[1] I will not address the topic of immigration in this work but I can say that my experience of the reality on the ground has been, "It is complicated." By and large I was working with many people who had been doing no more than seeking a better life for themselves. On the other hand, there was a population that was somewhat resentful of this "foreign invasion." Behind this there is a whole complex of political and economic factors beyond the control of the local populace, here and in Mexico. In the meantime I could see that US immigration law is a complicated morass that can only be applied arbitrarily and unevenly, such that one person who came to the country illegally is able to get legal status, but another is not and the only difference might be the curious technicalities of the law.

To put it mildly, the public school system has generally failed to teach the children the basics of reading and writing, or even the most elementary facts of history, whether of the United States or anywhere else, while it has inculcated a system of "values" wholly at odds with what the parents wished to inculcate at home. At best, it left the children without any guidance as to what it means to be a man or woman, while fostering a moral and intellectual environment that routinely stripped the children of the faith they received from their family.

Then, we move to social injustice in the realm of family life itself. I could see, in the people to whom I was ministering how the public acceptance of cohabitation and the facility of divorce undermined the stability of marriage at both ends. I knew that not just married women, but teenage girls were bombarded with propaganda pressuring them to use contraception. The immigrant women I knew generally liked being women and loved having children. Yet, when health problems arose, they were often bullied into sterilization—the cheap and easy solution—rather than helped to overcome the problem in a way that would enable them to continue having children.

This just scratches the surface when it comes to the ways in which social injustice impacted the life of my parishioners. These are certainly not the sort of things that usually come up with the topic of social injustice, but they are very real and pervasive.

Yes, there was racism too, but I would hardly have called it "systemic," unless specially targeting the Hispanic community for propaganda to take the Covid vaccines were to be regarded as "systemic racism."

As for economic injustice, my experience is that work was available for those who wanted it, and there was no lack of people who through hard work succeeded in raising their material standard of living. Indeed, most of the immigrant population seemed to enjoy a standard of living far in excess of that which they left behind.

Even those who lacked "documentation," despite the danger of deportation that weighed upon them, were often able to get good jobs and buy houses.

From a pastor's point of view, economic hardship was not so much the problem, not locally anyway, but the worldliness and loss of faith that went with economic prosperity.

From the perspective of a parish priest, then, social injustice is part of the pastoral "reality" one must face.

First of all, this brings a sense of powerlessness, as a pastor, to address the actual injustices, especially since law and public policy are shaped first of all on a national level and secondly by a left-wing Oregon state government, powered by the city of Portland.

Second, it becomes clear that this social injustice is the work of the "world" in the biblical sense, that is, the fruit of a society organized without and against God; this brings to the fore the conflict between the Gospel and this world.

The pastoral challenge, then, is to make people aware of this worldly reality and guide and strengthen them so that rather than merely letting themselves be carried along with the current, they might be able, like the salmon in the Columbia River, to swim against the current, thereby growing in faith and holiness, while passing that faith on to their children, despite the world.

The series of essays, then, which I originally wrote for the parish bulletin and which I now offer to the general public, was meant to nourish the faith of the people by making them aware of the challenges presented by the world in which they live, seeing those challenges in light of an integral exposition of the theme of social justice—the right ordering of human social life—which reveals thereby the vast disorder that surrounds us.

I will begin with the original essays on creation, which address the obstacle of the scientific mindset, which has undermined faith and excluded the word of God from

the "discussion." The consideration of creation will also
lay the foundation for the consideration of social justice,
first through the key role of the seventh day, the Sabbath,
which becomes the Lord's Day.

Then, when I enter the treatment of social justice
itself, I look to Eden for light as to the right ordering of
human social life. In Eden we find the fundamental orders
of human life: man beneath God, the interior order of
man himself, the relation between man and woman, and
mans' dominion over the physical world, which he was
given to *cultivate and care for.* [2]

In that light of the lost order of Eden, which is fully
restored in the first link, in relation to God, through the
redemptive work of Christ, I treat of right religion as the
foundation of the whole social order.

We could consider here the implications of what Pope
Benedict XVI once wrote:

> Worship, that is the right kind of cult, of rela-
> tionship with God, is essential for the right kind
> of human existence, in the world. It is so pre-
> cisely because it reaches beyond everyday life.
> Worship gives us a share in heaven's mode of
> existence, in the world of God, and allows light to
> fall from that divine world into ours..... It lays
> hold in advance of a more perfect life and, in so
> doing, gives our present life its proper measure. [3]

In this light, then, I go on to treat of marriage and
family, as the beginning and foundation of all human
society, then work and the environment in terms of man's
dominion over the physical world, and finally, I will enter
into the subject of government and the common good.

This book is not a "scholarly work," nor does it intend
to be complete and exhaustive. Rather it contains the

2   Gen. 2:15
3   Ratzinger, Joseph Cardinal, *The Spirit of the Liturgy.* San Francisco:
Ignatius Press, 2000, 21.

uncommon reflections of a parish priest. Nevertheless, these uncommon reflections challenge the narrative that we have generally been given, a narrative that sidelines the distinctive and essential contribution of the Church even to life in this world. These reflections seek to reclaim "social justice," which has become such a toxic expression, for the Church to which it belongs by right.

PART I

CREATION

EVERY SUNDAY WE RECITE TOGETHER: "I believe in one God, the Father almighty, maker of heaven and earth, of all things visible and invisible." Or in the Apostles' Creed: "I believe in God, the Father almighty, creator of heaven and earth." The doctrine of the creator and creation is not the whole of the creed, but it is the foundation for everything else. If we get this wrong, then, even if we still profess the rest of the creed, its meaning will have become distorted beyond recognition. Yet, there is probably no part of the creed that has been so subject to attack, distortion, and outright rejection over the course of the last century or more.

Before writing about creation directly from the standpoint of faith, we need to address what might be called the obstacles to faith. The first, of course, is the highly exaggerated regard for the importance and authority of "science."

1

Critique of Science

THE EXAGGERATED AUTHORITY OF SCIENCE IS AN OBSTACLE TO FAITH

The word "science" today evokes the most sure and authoritative kind of knowledge. It speaks of what is not just an opinion or conjecture, but "proven fact." It is identified with the work of human reason to such an extent that what is "scientific" is rational, and what is not supported by "science" is, at best, mere opinion, and at worst, irrational superstition.

Now, if we pay close attention, the status of what now goes by the name of "science," as the most sure and authoritative kind of knowledge, is not a proven fact, supported by science.[1] Indeed, if we examine the claim, we will see that it is, at best, misleading.

So what is "science"? Well it is surely the sort of knowledge that is produced by what is called the scientific method.

Using that handy contemporary research tool called "Google" we find that the expression is promptly defined thus: "A method of procedure that has characterized natural science since the 17th century, consisting in systematic observation, measurement, and experiment, and the formulation, testing, and modification of hypotheses."

The power of the method was perhaps shown most dramatically by Galileo in his famous experiment dropping different weights from the leaning tower of Pisa and showing by experiment that they hit the ground at

---

1 The word "science" comes from the Latin word *scientia* which simply means "knowledge" but was applied in particular to the most important form of knowledge, demonstrative knowledge. It used to include such things as "philosophical science" and "theological science."

the same time. "You say that the heavier weight will fall faster? Gotcha! See the two weights hit the ground at the same time." End of debate.

Nevertheless, it marks the beginning of a new debate because we still don't know why the weights fall at the same rate. That leads to a whole history of systematic observation, measurement, and experiment, and the formulation, testing, and *modification of hypotheses*. Curious, in the end the results are never certain, but always tentative, always subject to modification as more data becomes available.

More to the point though is what is implied and presupposed in the whole method.

To begin with, the systematic observation is driven by some question like, "Do different weights fall at the same rate or different rates?" That question presupposes some knowledge, namely that bodies have something called "weight" that gives them an inclination to fall. So our knowledge of the world never starts with science, but science presupposes that we live in an intelligible world about which we already know something.

Next, the whole process of systematic observation, measurement, and experiment shows that science is dealing with only a particular aspect of the world in which we live; science is only examining the world insofar as it falls within the realm of observation by our senses, either directly or by way of instruments we have fashioned to extend our perception. Further, science depends on measuring those observable aspects of reality, which means in some way putting a number to them and bringing them into the realm of mathematics.

This ends up being true even for sciences that touch on unique human realities like economics, psychology, sociology, and even history. In these areas statistics becomes the key to making these realities measurable in some way.

This method has been very powerful in its ability to produce results in terms of technology, but as far as understanding is concerned that is another matter. We could say that the focus on the measurable means that science touches only upon the most superficial aspect of reality.

So how does this bear on God and creation?

If the scientific method is taken as the only source of knowledge and the scientific method only examines measurable material reality, then by definition spiritual reality (God, the angelic world, and the human soul) is unknowable. If, further, it is supposed that only what is knowable exists, then the conclusion is that spiritual reality does not exist.

That, in a nutshell, is the argument for agnosticism and atheism. It claims to be supported by science and therefore by reason, but the whole argument relies on the non-scientific (and highly questionable) presupposition that the only way to knowledge is the scientific method.

During the past couple of centuries, at least, faith in the Creator has been undermined by a perceived conflict between faith and science. This perceived conflict really arises because of an exaggerated esteem for the value of science.

What we could call the "modern mentality" supposes that the scientific method is the only path to knowledge. Then, since the scientific method itself only treats of material measurable reality, it would follow that we cannot have any knowledge about any sort of non-material, spiritual reality. Finally, a further step to outright atheism is taken in the affirmation that what is unknowable does not exist.

Yet, as I already pointed out, the supposition that the scientific method is the only path to knowledge is not proven by science; it is an unproven and highly questionable supposition.

THE PERVASIVE CULTURE OF "FACT" AND "OPINION"

Nevertheless, that supposition is very pervasive in our culture and has a very powerful influence on the education of children. Children are taught from a very young age to distinguish between "fact" and "opinion."

That sounds like a no-brainer, right? Actually, it is an insidious byproduct of the exaltation of science over any other form of knowledge. You see, "fact" is defined by what is "proven," while anything else is relegated to the realm of mere opinion.

So, what is proven? Only the "facts" established by means of the scientific method. That means that every statement about God and spiritual reality can only be an "opinion." Further, every statement about right and wrong is also relegated to the realm of opinion. This is the source of moral relativism.

There is a further consequence of this division of all knowing between fact and opinion. Fact is judged to be so independent of what we might think about it, independent of whether we know it or not, independent of whether we agree or not. Fact is "objective." Opinion, however, depends on the person who holds the opinion and so is perceived as completely unconnected to the realm of objective fact. Opinion is seen as purely "subjective."

There is no criterion provided even to judge one opinion as better than another or one opinion as closer to fact than another. In the end, all opinion is equally worthless as far as reality is concerned; or all opinion is equally valid as far as the worth of the person is concerned.

Since all statements of meaning or value are mere opinions, all facts are devoid of meaning and value. Thus, we end up living in a world of meaningless facts, in which all meaning derives from subjective opinion. Even more, since this is the way we instruct our children in school, we raise our children to perceive the world in this way and to live in such a world. That means that any "values" parents wish to impart to their children are no more than the "opinion" of the parents.

The former Supreme Court Justice Anthony Kennedy enshrined in Constitutional law an affirmation that is

the consequence of this division of fact and opinion:
"At the heart of liberty is the right to define one's own
concept of existence, of meaning, of the universe, and of
the mystery of human life."[2]

What has happened is that science has been unable to
furnish man with any meaning in life, but man cannot
live without meaning. So, man must furnish his own
meaning, regardless of "facts." For meaning, facts do not
matter. Since meaning can only come from myself, the
worst sort of tyranny would be to have someone else
impose his meaning on me. I can only be free if I get to
define my "own concept of existence, of meaning, of the
universe, and of the mystery of human life."

In the end, the scientific culture provides no direction
for human life, but only furnishes the tools, the power,
that enables human beings to fashion the world anew
according to their own chosen meanings.

At least, that is the message that we are given. In truth,
it is no more than a contemporary version of the most
ancient of lies: *You will be like gods, knowing good and evil.*[3]

Really, though, where has this led us?

Consider the point we have reached now in our country.
Consider the shrillness of the arguments about things
that people hold as important. To call them "arguments"
is to give these contemporary shouting matches a dignity
they do not deserve. Instead of arguments we have slogans,
one-liners, memes, and "icons." Facts are not used for
understanding, but as stones or clubs, chosen according
to their usefulness for attacking an opponent. If the facts
available are not suitable, they can be readily twisted or
distorted, or altogether made up.

Real argument is not possible because there is no
basis in a common understanding of reality. It should
be evident by now that the different sides in the great
conflicts of our age live in radically different mental and

---

2 *Planned Parenthood v. Casey; Lawrence v. Texas*
3 Gen. 3:5

moral universes. Our culture provides no real means of communication. "Dialog" becomes just an instrument of manipulation. Meanwhile, the stakes are too high for anyone to let another network of made-up meaning prevail over his own. There can be no peace among the different man-made ideologies and idols.

Different Forms of Knowing

So, one of the distortions produced by the exaltation of science I described is the insidious distinction between "fact" and "opinion." It is one of these seemingly innocuous and evident "axioms" that already contains hidden the presuppositions of a thoroughgoing materialism. It leads to our curious cultural split between objective fact-based science, devoid of meaning, and moral relativism built on subjective man-made systems of meaning (effectively the new idolatry of ideologies).

Still, it is not enough to criticize. If the distinction between fact and opinion is deceptive and misleading, what sort of distinction should be made regarding different forms of knowing?

The classical distinction recognizes *understanding, knowledge, belief, opinion,* and *conjecture* or *suspicion.*[4] Each of these different forms of knowing is referred not to "facts" as the standard, but to reality and truth.

If we recall the limitations of the scientific method (measurable material reality) then we will realize that discrete scientific "facts" make up only a small part of the whole reality.

Further, we can observe that the fact-opinion distinction involves a confusion of categories. Fact refers to one aspect of reality that is known, while opinion refers to a way of knowing. That puts a sharp division between our knowing and reality that already contains the seeds of skepticism, as though all our knowing activity, mere "opinion," has nothing to do with reality.

4   *Summa Theologiae,* IIa-IIae, q. 2 a. 1.

In any case, the classic philosophical distinction sets reality and truth on one side, as what is known, and on the other side a variety of different ways in which the mind draws near to and attains certainty about reality. Reality exists independently of our minds, but not independently of the mind of God; our mind, however, exists for the sake of grasping the truth of reality, and was created by God to be proportioned to reality.

Understanding is the immediate grasp of truths that are evident to the mind without any need of proof. The most basic of these truths (a truth that is implicit in every thought and statement, even those which would seek to deny this truth) is that nothing can both be and not be at the same time and in the same way. There are also other basic truths such as the whole is greater than the part.

There are also some truths that might not be as immediately obvious but are indeed self-evident to our experience of the world in which we live. One is that we live in a world that is composed of different kinds of things like men, horses, rhinoceroses, fire ants, humming-birds, roses, oak trees, Venus flytraps, oysters, quartz crystals, limestone, gold, water, and oxygen.

Note these examples, chosen pretty much at random, run from very complex animals and plants down to simple elemental substances. The last-mentioned oxygen also shows that some kinds might not be immediately evident since oxygen has only been distinguished from the more evident "air" by way of scientific analysis. As for water, it was once thought to be one of the four elements, but it has since been discovered that it is composed of the simpler realities of hydrogen and oxygen.

Yet, while it is obvious that the whole is greater than the part, it is less obvious, but nevertheless true, that some kinds of whole are actually greater than the sum of their parts.[5]

---

5   If we consider the parts of a living organism as cells and organs, the whole organism is a reality that is greater than its mere organic structure.

The scientific mentality, however, has often made the mistake of trying to reduce reality to being nothing more than a composition of parts.

In any case, understanding is the foundation for all human knowledge of any kind. It is rooted in a basic grasp our mind has of reality, simply because that is what the mind does.

Sometimes understanding might go by the name of "common sense," except the latter has more to do with an individual's inborn ability to judge what is true and false. Real understanding, however, sometimes requires a great deal of work to distinguish between what is truly evident and what only appeared evident at first glance.

At first glance air appears to be a simple homogenous substance, but on closer analysis it turns out that it is a combination of different gasses, some simple, like oxygen, some composite, like carbon dioxide. Still, if there were not some things that were truly evident, we could never distinguish truth from falsehood.

Knowledge, while it sometimes refers to anything the mind grasps with any degree of certainty, is most properly the sort of knowledge that is made certain by means of proof. The Latin word for "knowledge" is *scientia*, the root of our word "science." So originally science referred to any sort of "proven" knowledge, but in modern times it has been limited to knowledge that has been proven by the "scientific" method.

The scientific method employs what is called "inductive logic." That means scientific proof moves from the evidence of individual, discrete facts, and tries to establish general "laws." For example, from the discrete facts of heavy bodies falling, science comes up with the law of gravity.

There is also deductive proof that moves from principles that are grasped by understanding and proceeds by what is called the "syllogism" to certain conclusions. For example: the power of reason is man's most noble power; the good of a thing consists in the fulfillment of its most noble power; therefore, the human good consists in the fulfillment of the rational power. That is not only a simple deductive proof, but also a deductive proof by means of the cause, namely the nobility of the rational power.

It is also possible to reason from effect to cause. In this way we can come to some rational knowledge of the existence of God as the first uncaused cause.

By means of *understanding* and *knowledge* the mind grasps reality without being moved one way or another by our will or emotions. These are truly objective forms of knowing, yet we are still involved as the one who knows.

In the remaining forms of knowing the will plays an important part in the act of knowing; there is therefore an element of "subjectivity." This is not a bad thing, so long as we are cognizant of the role of the will, and so long as the will itself is rightly ordered with regard to reality.

Belief is the first form of knowing that involves the will. In belief the will moves the person to judge something as true on the authority of someone else.

Understanding and knowledge are forms of certain knowledge, but so is *belief*. Through understanding and knowledge, however, the mind can be said to "see" the truth of the matter.

Because we are necessarily social beings, our knowing is never wholly independent because in a variety of ways we are reliant on the testimony of others for knowledge of reality. We believe countless matters without ever questioning them and it could scarcely be otherwise.

Belief is certain because we do not question the source; if the source comes into question then the belief is shaken. So belief, finally, is only as good as the authority on which we rely. The better we judge the reliability of a source, the better founded will be our beliefs. Authority has no place in understanding and knowledge, but authority is decisive for belief.

Belief in God, however, is most reasonable and most sure, because he can neither deceive nor be deceived. He is the absolute source of all reality and all truth. Supernatural faith, which rests on the authority of God who reveals, is more certain than understanding or knowledge, even though it does not make us see the truth of what we believe.

Opinion differs from belief because opinion sees arguments on both sides, but judges that the weight of evidence lies on one side rather than the other. The conclusion is not proven, but to our mind it seems more likely. All opinions, then, are not equal. The better opinion is founded on better evidence and the better argument. So, the person who is a better judge of evidence and arguments will usually have better opinions. That means his opinions are more likely to be true to reality.

Unlike belief, with opinion the affirmation of one side of an argument does not rest on authority, but on what seems more probable to our mind. The more that "probability" rests on a good evaluation of arguments, the less opinions are reliant on mere emotion.

Nevertheless, emotion and will also contribute to swaying the mind one way or another in matters of opinion. That is because the evaluation of the quality of arguments will involve what seems good to a person; that apprehension of the good is connected with a person's will and emotions. Still, emotions are not all the same. Emotions themselves relate, more or less remotely, to reality. As a consequence, the more a person has a rightly ordered emotional life, the better his opinions will be. The person whose emotions are disordered and confused will be more likely to give way to questionable opinions.

Finally, *conjecture* or *suspicion* holds to the weaker argument, but the will inclines the mind to accept the matter for some reason extrinsic to the argument itself. The jealous husband suspects his wife of infidelity based on some trivial detail and despite his wife's countless displays of love and affection. On the other hand, in a positive way, a soldier in war suspects a booby trap because of some tiny detail that looks out of place.

This consideration of different forms of knowing points us to the whole of classical philosophy as an enterprise much broader and more varied than modern science. Many scientists, like the late Stephen Hawking, are great scientists but poor philosophers. Further, they do not know when they are departing from science and entering into philosophy. Much of what passes as "science" in the popular realm, especially in matters connected to faith, is actually poor philosophic interpretation of the meaning of scientific facts.

THE POWER OF THE SCIENTIFIC IMAGE OF REALITY

While I have been critical of the dominance of the "scientific mentality" it is important to keep in mind here that science, as such, is a legitimate means of inquiry; the problem is found rather in the reduction of all knowledge to science, which readily entails the reduction of all reality to that which is material and measurable.

For all that an image of reality emerged from the early scientific discoveries that has been quite powerful, quite hostile to faith, but which has itself become rather scientifically dated.

As recently as maybe 1900, science gave an image of the world that did indeed seem to favor atheism over belief in God. At that time, science was providing such a simple, seemingly self-contained picture of the universe that it could be easy to conclude that there was no need for God.

On the level of astrophysics, everything seemed to be simply explained by Newton's principles of mass, inertia, and gravity. On the chemical level, everything seemed neatly explained by the simplicity of atoms and their combinations—the electron, the first subatomic particle, was only discovered in 1897. Plant and animal life was explained in terms of cell theory and the interior of cells was thought to be nothing more than a sort of generic protoplasm. Finally, Darwin's theory of evolution seemed to give an explanation to the origin of life itself. Science, it was thought, had explained everything. What was left unexplained was insignificant. No room appeared to be left for God.

Here, though, we already run into the difference between scientific facts and their philosophical interpretation. Even with this very simple and, by today's standards, primitive science, there is no explanation of why the laws governing astrophysics, chemistry, and biology should be such as they were, nor why anything should exist in the first place. That was all simply taken as a given.

The 20th century, however, witnessed a new explosion of scientific discoveries, with startling developments like relativity, quantum mechanics, and genetics.

The new developments revealed an extraordinary and intricate complexity of order on every level of the universe, from the vast expanse of the light years through which innumerable galaxies are spread, to the intricacies of subatomic particles, to the amazing interior complexity and order of cells.

A few simple points can be made about all this.

First, this brought an end to the rational pretensions of what is called "determinism."

Basically, the mentality of determinism, which underlay the scientific mentality from the beginning, holds that the universe as we know it has developed purely in a predetermined fashion according to fixed laws. Consequently, if we could only know the original state of the universe and the laws that held at that time, we could accurately predict everything that has happened since, or ever will happen. On this view, the only possible place left for God was to get the whole process started. After that he becomes irrelevant.

The uncertainty principle of quantum mechanics blew determinism out of the water.[6]

---

6   In quantum mechanics the "uncertainty principle" states that the more precisely the position of some particle is determined, the less precisely its momentum can be predicted from initial conditions,

The uncertainty principle also makes it much harder to believe that the complex order of the universe could be the result of pure chance; rather it calls for the guidance of the whole process by some sort of "super-intelligence."

The very different intricacies that govern the vast regions of space, the internal mechanisms of particles, and dynamism of living things strongly suggests that more complex realities are not simply reducible to being a sum of their simplest parts, as was once thought. Irreducibility not only throws into question the doctrine of evolution, but points to those complex realities as being intended by a maker, rather than just spit out at the end of a process of random change.

In other words, if a horse is just the sum of its parts, then it is not too far of a stretch to imagine it as somehow developing from the random interactions of those tiny parts. If, however, a horse is a whole that possesses its own nature and integrity beyond those parts, then the interactions of parts, which is really all that science examines, cannot explain its origin. Rather, it possesses an inherent intelligibility that is proper to something that is made by an intelligent maker.

The argument or at least suggestion becomes even stronger when we realize that a horse, apart from possessing its own integrity as a whole, is integrated in a remarkable way into a larger ecological whole.

Finally, we learn that all this order and complexity fits together perfectly to allow for the most improbable result of all: intelligent human life on planet earth.

Copernicus was thought to have revolutionized the way we thought about ourselves as human beings, because

---

and vice versa. This is related to the "observer effect" that notes that measurements of certain systems cannot be made without effecting that system. Because of the uncertainty principle, the predictive power of science, in quantum mechanics, becomes a matter of probability; while the observer effect shows the limits of measurement and the presence of a certain subjectivity in the very means (measurement) that was supposed to establish the objectivity of science.

we no longer saw ourselves as being at the center of the universe. So, the scientific mentality dethroned man from his royal status, we could say. Yet, through what is called the "anthropic principle," man has been placed right back at the center of the physical universe in a new and unforeseen way.[7] All of this vast complex order has been fortuitously (or should we say providentially) arranged so that we could be here.

Now none of these conclusions about intelligent design are scientific facts, but philosophical conclusions drawn from (or at least suggested by) the scientific evidence.

My point here is that while in 1900 the atheistic opinion might have seemed reasonable, in 2023 the atheistic opinion has really become very flimsy and tenuous. Still, the popular imagination has not developed with the development of science. In the popular imagination it still seems as though science favors atheism.

DIFFERENT KINDS OF STORIES; DIFFERENT KINDS OF INTERPRETATION

After writing about the limitations of modern science and giving a fuller view of human knowing through the distinction among understanding, knowledge, belief, opinion, and suspicion or conjecture, I wrote about how the scientific developments of the past century tend to favor more the opinion of "intelligent design" than that of atheistic belief. Nevertheless, atheistic belief retains a strong hold on the popular imagination of science.

Key to this underlying atheistic belief is not the facts, but the philosophical interpretation—or bad philosophical interpretation. The philosophical interpretations are communicated to the popular imagination by way of "stories."

---

7   The anthropic principle may be more of an observation than a true principle; it is the observation that built into the universe are a whole set of statistical improbabilities, without which intelligent life on earth would have been impossible.

So it might be good to consider the relation between different kinds of stories and the truth and facts.

You see there are fact-based stories that are true and there are fact-based stories that are false. There are also stories that are true, even though they are not factual. There are also stories that are neither factual nor true.

Consider stories that might be told about George Washington.

A story that tells us that George Washington was a land surveyor and slave owner, but says nothing more, would be factual, but false. It gives us a picture of George Washington that is not true to the real historical person.

A story that tells of George Washington, the father of our country, leader of the Continental Army during the War of Independence and the 1st President of the United States, while omitting the fact that he owned slaves, would be true, but not complete.

Then there is the story about George Washington, chopping down the cherry tree and confessing the deed to his father, saying, "I cannot tell a lie." The story is not factual but tells either the truth about the character of George Washington, or what Americans have wanted to believe about his character. In the latter case it reveals a truth about American values and ideals.

Then there is the children's story, "George Washington Rabbit," which, apart from the name, has nothing whatsoever to do with George Washington.

There can also be stories that are mixtures of fact and fiction. For example, an historical novel about the life of George Washington might contain many facts about George Washington, mixed in with material that is made up for the sake of the story. The truth of the story would not be judged so much on the proportion of fact and fiction, but on whether or not it was true to George Washington's character and historical importance.

There is yet another type of historical novel, that uses history (say the American revolution and Founding period) as a backdrop for the fictional story with its fictional characters. Such a story may or may not contain a true meaning and it may or may not be true to the history that serves as a backdrop for the action.

So how does the "scientific story" fit in here?

Roughly the popular story runs like this: In the beginning there was a big explosion of light and energy; from there the universe went expanding and cooling; as parts of the universe cooled, gaseous matter came together and stars were formed and from the stars planets came forth; some planets had the right conditions for water to form and from water life came; this happened on planet earth; after life came from the water it gradually evolved over time; from plant life, animal life developed, and from animal life came the conscious intelligent life of human beings. The End.

This is the story that is told in our schools and presented simply as "the scientific truth" and the explanation for everything.

Nevertheless, factual as the story may be, it actually explains nothing. All it does is give us a sequence of events. The addition of physical laws would provide some connection between the events. Still, there is no explanation for why these laws and not others, no explanation for why anything exists at all, and no meaning and purpose to the things that do exist and the sequence of events. Most of all, it gives the illusion of explaining the universe without God but fails to do so precisely because of what is taken for granted and left unexplained.

In the end, this popular scientific account is rather like the George Washington, land surveyor and slave owner story; it is factual but leaves out what is most important about the universe.

The story could be retold in a very different manner. In the beginning God said, "Let there be light" and there was a big explosion of light and energy. And God guided that light and energy according to the laws that he inscribed in nature so that the universe went expanding and cooling; as parts of the universe cooled, gaseous matter came together and stars were formed and from the stars planets came forth. God guided this process so that in one corner of the universe, on the planet earth, water was formed, and from water God brought forth all manner of life that developed over time. In this way God created both plants and animals. Finally, God created man, endowed with intelligence and free will, in his own image.

This story is based on the same scientific facts as the more popular story. It bears some resemblance to the 1st chapter of Genesis. It still leaves some big questions about meaning and purpose unanswered.

And what about the 1st chapter of Genesis? What kind of story does it tell?

2

Genesis

THE TRUE STORY OF GENESIS

We turn our attention now to the 1st chapter of Genesis, which tells the story of creation. By faith we accept the story as true, revealed by God who can neither deceive nor be deceived. Just because we accept the story as true, that does not yet tell us how it relates to the facts. Is the story true the way a myth can be true, because it conveys a true meaning, or is the story true the way a fact-based story is true, because of both the facts and the meaning? Or is the matter a little more complicated?

So let's start with the evident facts. The 1st chapter of Genesis speaks to us of the basic facts of a world with which we are all familiar. We readily recognize the sky, the sea, the land, the sun, the moon, the stars, the plants, the animals, and man. Indeed, in a general way, everything is complete and nothing is missing from the picture.

Children will often ask about dinosaurs. Well, dinosaurs are land animals that were created by God on the 6th day, so they too are accounted for in the narrative.

The 1st chapter of Genesis also tells us that this entire world, "heaven and earth," was created by God. That is not a "scientific fact," because it does not fall into the scope of science, but we could call it a philosophical and religious fact.

It is a religious fact because it is revealed by God, but it is also a philosophical fact because it can be grasped in some measure by human reason.

The word of God points this out. In the Old Testament we read: *From the greatness and beauty of created things, their original author, by analogy, is seen.*[1] And, in the New Testament, *Ever since the creation of the world, God's invisible attributes*

---

1 Wisd. 13:5

of eternal power and divinity have been able to be understood and perceived in what he has made. [2]

In other words, the human mind is capable of arriving at some sort of knowledge of God's existence, power, and beauty by way of a consideration of the created world. That is a work not of scientific reason, which examines the mechanisms and structures of created things, but of philosophical reason, which examines more the natures, meaning, and origin of things.

Where we have stumbled in the modern era is by assuming that everything in the story of Genesis, everything about the way the story is told, is also "fact," fact like scientific and historical fact. The real stumbling block for our mind is the seven-day structure of the narrative.

Some will think that the Bible is asserting as "fact" that God created the world in six twenty-four hour "days." That is a supposed "fact" that is easily addressed once we grasp that the Hebrew word "yom," which is properly translated as "day," can refer to a more indeterminate period of time.

That still leaves us with the problem of the order of the days. Some people will then try to reconcile Genesis and scientific fact by showing how the development of the world in the six days actually matches the order of development shown to us by science. Not only do these efforts run into problems with the actual text of Genesis, but they also raise the question, "Are we missing the point?" Was God's intention and the intention of the sacred author really a matter of revealing the secrets of cosmic history that would later be discovered by science?

Before the age of scientific discovery, it was common among Christians to assume both the 24-hour day and the order of the days as "fact." Despite certain difficulties in the text, there didn't seem to be any overriding reason to the contrary. So, some Fathers of the Church, like St. Basil the Great (4th century), commented on Genesis on the basis of that assumption.

---

2   Rom. 1:20

Nevertheless, at least one ancient Father of the Church, St. Augustine (4th to 5th century), took a very different approach to what he referred to as the literal interpretation of Genesis.[3] He saw the seven days neither as 24-hour periods nor as an order of time as we know it, but as divisions of angelic knowledge of the created world. The "periods" of knowledge might be successive, but the reality of the created world was simultaneous. It would be as though we were to look at a painting first as a whole, then, in our mind, divide it into parts, and finally examine the details in each part. The painting, with all its parts and details was always there complete, but our examination passed through successive stages.

I will not delve any further into St. Augustine's interpretation, which I think is the best, but we have seen enough to pass over the stumbling block of the structure of seven days. It is more a vehicle of narrative meaning, than a factual element (in either a modern scientific or historical sense) of the story.

The Main Message of the Creation Story of Genesis

We are now ready to take a look at the actual meaning of the creation story of Genesis. We need to begin with the fundamental truths that are revealed in the story—the principal message—before moving to some of the more subtle messages.

First, God is revealed as both the one who creates everything and gives form, structure, and distinction to all created things.

Second, in all the visible creation, man (male and female) has a special status and dignity because he is created according to the image and likeness of God.

Let's start then with the very fact and reality of creation. *In the beginning God created heaven and earth.*[4] The Hebrew expression "heaven and earth" simply refers to everything

---

3 St. Augustine, *De Genesi ad Litteram Libri Duodecim*; the matter of angelic knowledge is synthesized by St. Thomas Aquinas, *Summa Theologiae* (*ST*), Ia, q. 56–57.
4 Gen. 1:1

that exists that is not God himself, what we call "the universe," except that finally "heaven and earth" also includes what we refer to in the Creed as "all things visible and invisible."

That means that there is God and then there is everything else.

Everything else is dependent upon God for its very existence; had God decided not to create, nothing else would have existed. Because we exist and because we live in a world of things that exist, day in and day out, we tend to take all these things for granted. We tend to assume that the things that are must be. We are mistaken.

Some modern-day philosophers have tried to set this truth before people's minds by way of a dramatic question: Why is there something rather than nothing?

The philosopher's question points us very clearly to another aspect of the meaning of creation: God creates out of nothing.

When we make something, we take materials that already exist and we refashion them. We might reshape things and join them together, as a carpenter builds a cabinet. Or we might make use of the natural properties of things to change the ingredients into something new, like wheat into bread. When God creates, however, he gives existence to the whole thing, matter and form.

So far, we have been considering what God creates (the everything else), but that leads us back to God himself, the Creator.

People will often ask, "Who made God?" The question is misplaced. It arises because we are used to the things that, precisely because they were created, demand a reason for their existence. If we saw God face to face, so to speak, we could not even ask the question; it would not occur to us. If we truly knew God as he is, his existence would be self-explanatory.

So when Moses asked God his name, God said, *I am who am.*[5] One meaning of that cryptic expression is: "I am

---

5   Exod. 3:14

the one who is, who exists of and by himself, without any cause; I am the one who is existence; everything else has existence and it has existence because I gave it to them."

Now in this life we do not know God as he is in himself, but only through the things that he has made. That is why he remains hidden from us and why, even though we cannot doubt the existence of the things that he has made, we can actually doubt the existence of the Creator himself.

Yet, once we consider well that there is on one side God who creates and on the other everything that he created, that is completely dependent on the Creator for its existence, then we can also realize that God is not any created thing, nor is he like any created thing. "Between Creator and creature no similitude can be expressed without implying an even greater dissimilitude."[6]

The dissimilitude is greater, but "We can name God by taking his creatures' perfections as our starting point, 'for from the greatness and beauty of created things comes a corresponding perception of their Creator.'"[7]

What we can name, we can know in some fashion. So even though God surpasses or transcends all creatures, we can have true knowledge of him because of the dependence of creature on the Creator, because we know that the Creator is not the creature, and because all that is good, beautiful, and perfect in creatures comes from the Creator and so is found in him in an infinitely higher manner.[8]

So God is not the biggest bully on the block, he is not some extra-terrestrial race that has somehow programmed human evolution, he is not some old man with a white beard sitting on a cloud, he is not the greatest super-computer ever made, he is not some mysterious radiance of light, nor is he some hidden energy or force.

---

6   Lateran Council IV, quoted in the Catechism of the Catholic Church (CCC) 43.

7   CCC 41, Wisd. 13:5

8   Cf. *ST*, Ia, q. 13

He did create all things by the wisdom of his mind
and the power of his will. That divine mind embraces
in one single simple act of knowing everything that all
the scientists of the world have ever discovered and have
yet to discover, everything that all the philosophers have
ever thought or will think, everything that every single
human being from the beginning to the end of time has
perceived with their senses, fashioned in their imagination,
or thought with their mind, and all that human knowledge
is little more than a drop of water in the ocean of God's
immense wisdom.[9]

Now the doctrine of "creation out of nothing" means
also that time itself is a created reality and that God stands
completely outside of time—that is the real meaning of
God's eternity.

"Creation out of nothing" does not mean that there
had to be a beginning of time, but this truth is revealed
in the first words of Genesis, *in the beginning.* God not
only created time, he created a beginning of time. This
is supported, but not proven, by the scientific theory of
the "Big Bang."

The beginning of time certainly highlights the reality
of creation and the radical dependence of the creature
upon God.

Nevertheless, it is important to grasp that just as things
did not have to exist in the first place, they did not have
to exist in this way.

The fact of things now existing and the fact that they
exist as they do is so immediately evident to us it is hard
to conceive of them existing in any other way.

Scientific theories, at least until the development of
quantum mechanics and the principle of uncertainty,
reinforced this way of thinking because of the underlying attitude of philosophical determinism. Philosophical
determinism is the philosophical doctrine that everything

---

9   Cf. *ST*, Ia, q. 14-21

in the world developed according to the strict necessity
of determined laws.

Genesis reveals that God chose to create the universe
(he didn't have to do it) and chose to create it the way it
is (he didn't have to do it this way).

Genesis also reveals that the created universe is good
in the judgment of God. *God saw that it was good.*

There is an error called "voluntarism" that holds that
goodness is so completely dependent on God's will that
if God had willed the things we understand to be evil
to be good, then they would be good. If God had willed
murder to be good, then it would have been good. The
words of Genesis, *God saw that it was good,* correct this error
by relating the goodness in creation to God's knowledge
and wisdom, not directly to his will.

Created reality is good, but the word of God does not
teach that the universe is perfect in every way (actually
absolute perfection can only be found in God himself) nor
is it "the best of possible worlds." Actually, if we consider
well the word of God, we will realize that the universe
in its present form is—as should be obvious—imperfect
and, less obviously, provisional. The present imperfect
universe is, we could say, a path to a universe that will be
perfect in its kind, when God himself brings all things
to completion.

The goodness of the universe is revealed precisely in
what are called the "works of distinction." Genesis first tells
us that God created the universe but presents the world to
us as *a formless wasteland.*[10] There then follows the sequence
of six days in which the heaven, the sea, the earth, and *all
their array* are fashioned.[11] Each day God pronounces his
work "good'" and declares the whole *very good.*[12]

Existence itself is a good, but mere existence, we could
say is the least of created goods. Created things achieve

10   Gen. 1:1
11   Cf. Gen. 2:1
12   Gen. 1:31

their goodness through being distinguished from one another, each according to its kind, each "obeying" as it were the laws of its kind.

The formless, limitless wasteland of mere existence is not called good. The things that are defined and limited, we could say, each according to its kind, are good. This is the general judgment of antiquity: goodness for created things does not come through being infinite, shapeless, formless, without limits, but precisely through proper definition, shape, and form. Created goodness arises from proper measure, definite form, and right order. Created beauty is constituted by integrity (or having all the requisite parts), proportion among the parts, and clarity.

Through their proper limits and forms created things are good and beautiful according to their kinds, but their goodness and beauty is thereby limited and imperfect. They are creatures, not God.

Modern society, however, has been characterized by rejection of limits, hatred of form, and disorder. It is as though modern man, in his rebellion against God, in wanting to be like God without God, wants to return to the primeval chaos of a formless wasteland. This becomes love of weirdness. So modern art moves towards formlessness or clashing of forms or forms that clash with reality: nothing fits.

CREATION AND THE PROBLEM OF EVIL

The first chapter of Genesis, by and large, reveals God's completed work, which is pronounced "good" in its parts and "very good" as a whole. Nevertheless, from what follows we learn how sin enters the world, giving rise to a whole history, marked by sin, suffering, and death, a history that would truly be tragic were it not for the redemption wrought by our Lord Jesus Christ.

I noted that just because creation is "very good" that does not mean that it is perfect in every way or the best of possible worlds. Actually, only God himself is perfect in every way.

The very imperfection of creation is what gives rise to the possibility of evil. Something more needs to be said as to how that possibility is implicit in the account of creation. We must always keep in mind, though, that God who made all things good, does not cause evil. Rather, by making things the way he did God allowed for both the possibility and the reality of evil.

Within the six days it is important to note that God creates different kinds of trees and plants, bearing fruit, containing seeds, and reproducing themselves; different kinds of birds and sea creatures that reproduce themselves; different kinds of land animals that reproduce themselves. Likewise man, in the image of God, reproduces himself.

We see here the truth taught by St. Thomas Aquinas that God not only gives to creatures the goodness of being like him through the fact of their existence, but he also gives to them the goodness of being like him through their being causes of good within the created order.[13] Existence comes straight from God, but insofar as things come forth from other creatures by way of created causality, like reproduction, they do not come straight from God.

God's causality never fails, but created causality does. Even apart from the question of moral evil, there will be deficiencies in a created world in which one creature acts upon another and where different creatures are dependent on each other in various ways. That happens simply because creatures, not being God, are limited and imperfect.

As for moral evil two things in the first chapter give us a hint of what is to come.

First, among all the things that God calls good, there is one thing mentioned on the first day that is excluded from that judgment: On the first day God judges the light as "good," but then he separates the darkness from the light. He never calls the darkness of the first day "good." St. Augustine interprets this in terms of spiritual

---

13   Cf. *ST*, Ia, q. 103, a. 6

light and darkness and sees here an indication of the rebellion that took place within the angelic world. All the angels were created "good," filled with spiritual light, but some of those angels freely rejected that light and became "darkness." God judged the darkness separating it from the light.

The imperfect universe, created by God, by allowing created freedom, also allows for the possibility of moral evil.

When God creates man, male and female, he speaks to them, giving them a command: *Be fruitful and multiply; fill the earth and subdue it. Have dominion over the fish of the sea, the birds of the air, and all the living things that move on earth.*[14] The fact of the command implies the presence of human freedom and therefore the possibility of sin.

Now today, we often meet with the claim, "God made me this way. Therefore, it must be good." At best this is a very deceptive and misleading claim.

First of all, by our own free choices, we have made ourselves in certain ways, we have developed certain habits, definite ways of acting and thinking that, had we made different choices, would have been different. Virtue or vice becomes for us a kind of second nature of our own making.

Further, while our souls come directly from God, our bodies with their natural dispositions are formed by the natural process of human procreation (or, tragically for some, the laboratory process of 'in vitro fertilization'). God fashions our bodies through intermediate causes, with their imperfections.

Further, from an early age, the lower part of our soul, imagination, memory, and emotion, is profoundly shaped by social influences from parents, to school, to friends (not to mention television, internet, and social media) before we ever reflect on the matter.

None of this determines us one way or another, but it sets up the context in which our free choices will be made. They give us certain dispositions and inclinations,

14   Gen. 1:28

some towards what is truly good, some not so good, and some disordered.

Evil—it should be noted—is not so much a positive reality as a disorder, a lack of the order to the good that should be there. We could call it a tendency to fall back into the nothingness from which we were created.

Finally, and this is a message contained in the rest of the Bible, God only allows evil because he is capable of bringing forth from the very evil a much greater good. Making a saint from a sinner is actually a greater work than creating something from nothing.

The Collect for the Mass of the 26th Sunday of Ordinary Time calls upon "God, who manifest your almighty power above all by pardoning and showing mercy...."

THE SPECIAL STATUS OF MAN IN CREATION: UNDER ATTACK IN THE MODERN WORLD

The first main thing to consider in the Genesis narrative of creation is the simple fact of creation and the meaning of the distinction of things and their goodness. Now we must turn our attention to the second main point of the creation narrative, the special status of man, created male and female, in the image and likeness of God.

In today's world the special status of man has been under a sustained attack for more than a century, indeed since the time of Charles Darwin. Whatever else might be said about the theory of evolution, it has been used to deny that human beings belong to a higher order than the animals.

Human intelligence is seen as no more than an accidental byproduct of evolution that may have made us to be more powerful than other animals, but does not otherwise elevate us above them, or characterize us as having a more noble nature. Scientists will spend a great deal of effort trying to show that the most developed among other animals (e.g., chimpanzees and dolphins) truly have intelligence. Indeed, the language of intelligence is readily applied to all sorts of animals, without any clear idea of what makes human beings different. Where there is no evidence of intelligence some people are quite ready to affirm that we might just not understand their language. Following this line of thinking, birds might be having very sophisticated conversations, we just don't understand them.

The concept of justice actually reveals the uniqueness of human intelligence, because through the concept of justice we grasp an invisible order of relationships among persons and things that transcends both pleasure and utility. The concept of beauty also reveals the character of human intelligence, because it shows that we are capable of simply admiring a person or thing for what it is, not what we can get out of it. Some animals might exhibit a sort of curiosity, but not admiration.

Nevertheless, on the political front we now have the "animal rights" movement, which is not just about humane treatment of animals, but declaring the equality of species. Therefore, animals must have rights just like we do, even equal rights. In 2018 a lawsuit was filed in Washington County, Oregon on behalf of a horse against its previous owner, seeking damages for neglect. Fortunately, some measure of sanity remains, as the judge deemed the horse did not have legal standing and so dismissed the lawsuit. Nevertheless, as of this writing the dismissal has been appealed.

We could perhaps distinguish two major, distinct, yet intertwined threads of the environmentalist movement, the scientific thread and the religious thread, which following the "Gaia hypothesis" moves towards a sort of worship of the earth and of "mother nature."

Religious environmentalism does not only seek to impede and avoid ongoing degradation of the environment for the sake of human life, but rather tends to see humans as the enemy and wants to make the world safe from humans.

Religious environmentalism reacts both against the technological society and the Christian faith. Indeed, because of the 1st chapter of Genesis, in particular the passage in which God says to men, *Fill the earth and subdue it. Have dominion over the fish of the sea, the birds of the air, and all the living things that move on the earth*, religious environmentalism typically blames Christianity for the degradation of the environment.[15]

In truth, the modern degradation of the environment results from the drive to conquer nature that began only in 16th century Europe. At that time, it was not very safe openly to proclaim atheism, but the roots of the drive for the conquest of nature were truly atheistic.

We need to consider some of the origins of this characteristic modern spirit of conquest and domination and where it has led us.

We can start with the Italian, Niccolò Machiavelli (died 1527), who regarded fortune, not providence, as the master of human affairs, who urged princes to do whatever they deemed necessary to acquire and maintain political power, insisting that it was necessary for them to seem good rather than really be good, outwardly to practice the religion of their people, but not inwardly believe or obey. If you want "toxic masculinity" Machiavelli likened fortune to a woman and said, "It is better to be impetuous than cautious, because fortune is a woman; and it is necessary, if one wants to hold her down, to beat her and strike her down."[16]

Then we move to the Englishman, Francis Bacon (died 1626), who applied the spirit of Machiavelli to the conquest of nature, putting that conquest, whether wittingly or unwittingly, at the service of the princes—consider how much technological advance has been driven by military needs or how much gets co-opted for either military power or the control of a populace.

Bacon wrote:

---

15 Gen. 1:28
16 Machiavelli, *The Prince*, XXV

> With regard to the mass and composition of it
> [natural history]: I mean it to be a history not
> only of nature free and at large (when she is left
> to her own course and does her work her way)
> .... but much more of nature under constraint
> and vexed; that is to say, when by art and the
> hand of man she is forced out of her natural state,
> and squeezed and moulded .... [for] the nature
> of things betrays itself more readily under the
> vexations of art than in its natural freedom.[17]

Bacon did not regard nature as good and benevolent, but as stingy and capricious. He saw no good in understanding nature "free and at large," left to her own course; he saw no good in admiring the work of God in nature and giving praise to the Creator; rather he thought that nature was to be constrained and vexed, squeezed and moulded, forced in spite of herself to do the will of men. Bacon and other like-minded thinkers forged the spirit that would drive the engine of the scientific and technological revolution.

One of Bacon's most famous statements was: "Knowledge is power." The goal of power was really to push God aside and fashion a paradise for man on earth.

It is important to make a couple observations here.

The problem is neither with science nor technology as such, but with the drive to conquer and dominate nature that has driven the scientific and technological revolutions. That drive to conquer and dominate has not recognized or accepted any limits, nor has it brooked any delays. So, what we see around us today is a world of uncontrolled and destructive industrial and technological growth.

That leads to another problem. It was easier to build the technological society than it is now to control it; indeed, it seems now to be beyond our control. We have now made ourselves dependent on our own inventions. We

---

17   Bacon, *The Great Instauration*, 25.

now consume vast amounts of energy, but could human life
any longer be sustained without vast energy consumption?
Could energy consumption be effectively reduced without
introducing extreme measures of control, measures that
put immense power into the hands of a few who have
not particularly shown themselves to be trustworthy?

That leads us back to the doctrine of Bacon, "Knowledge is power," the power of humanity has been expo-
nentially multiplied, but there has been no corresponding
advance in the justice of human beings. Indeed, underlying
much social, political, and economic organization is, we
could say, the attempt to build a sort of "machinery" of
prosperity that can function independently of the justice
of the human parts.

This line of reasoning argues that if we build self-driving
cars, then road safety will no longer be dependent upon
the carelessness or bad will of human drivers. The impe-
tus for self-driving cars is in the end a move to remove
one more activity, driving, from the realm of personal
responsibility and the vagaries of moral character.

THE TRUE CHRISTIAN SPIRIT OF STEWARDSHIP, CONTEMPLATION, AND PRAISE

So, the destructive spirit of modern conquest and domination is rightly criticized by the religious environmentalists, but it is altogether wrong to blame Christianity
for that spirit, even if Christians have blindly gone along
for the ride. In doing so, Christians have been taken in
and deceived by a spirit that is opposed to the truth and
reality of the faith. Christians have been taken in and
deceived by a spirit that in practice denies the existence
of the providential Creator and Ruler of the universe.

Religious environmentalism, on the other hand, has
effectively accepted the modern destruction of human
nature, and by means of reviving a new nature worship
has revived the spirit of ancient paganism, which threatens
to enslave man anew to the elements of the created world.

The true Christian spirit, which was evident in the Middle Ages despite the many sins and failings of men, saw the created world as the handiwork of the Creator, almost a second sacred Scripture, that should lead us to seek understanding, leading to admiration and the praise of God.

The dominion given to man over the created world was a sacred stewardship under God. Man must first master himself, live within the limits of his own created nature, subordinate to God, then understand the world created by God and serve as God's vice-regent, guiding raw nature to its perfection.

Because man is indeed tasked with bringing the created world to a sort of perfection, some sort of technological growth and advancement is indeed implied. Nevertheless, this would not be the sort we have experienced in the past few centuries, which has sought rather to suppress than to guide and perfect nature.

The uncontrolled growth we have actually experienced has made life to be rather comfortable—for a great many of us—in numerable ways. This makes it hard to criticize the process while enjoying the comfort, even though we are aware that the comfort has come with a steep price tag. It would be better to recognize that many of the comforts that we now enjoy are as chains to be lamented rather than a matter for rejoicing and boasting.

St. Augustine once wrote: "Those who are better able to endure want should think of themselves as richer on that account; for it is better to need little than to have much."[18] Unfortunately, we have now fashioned for ourselves many new needs.

The scientific revolution was born during the age of discovery. Here it would be good to observe opposing spirits in the discovery of America, one akin to the spirit of conquest that has driven the scientific revolution, the other was the spirit of evangelization. The spirit of conquest effectively sought to enslave the indigenous peoples of America; the spirit of evangelization sought to elevate them by means of the Gospel.

These days, "Columbus Day" gets replaced by "Indigenous Peoples Day," as though the indigenous peoples were living in a true Eden and had no need of the Gospel. Evangelists are judged no differently from the Conquistadors, while religious environmentalists look to indigenous peoples for their ideal of humanity. In the new myth of the fall of man, man in Eden does not sin, rather, the Eden of the Americas was invaded by evil men from Europe and the holy and innocent population was subjugated by the evil Europeans and their false religion of Christianity.

The Virgin of Guadalupe, Mother of the True God, Creator of Heaven and Earth, thought differently and taught the peoples of Mexico to receive the good inheritance of the Spaniards, despite the depredations of the conquistadors. We should learn to apply the teaching of Our Lady of Guadalupe in order to recover our Catholic tradition, purified of the false currents of modernism.

She teaches us that *whatever we do, in word or in deed, we should do everything in the name of the Lord Jesus, giving thanks to God the Father through him.*[19] This shows us the right purpose of all created things.

MAN: CREATED IN THE IMAGE OF GOD

The high point of the first six days, we could say, is the creation of man, male and female, in the image of God, but the special status of man has been under an intense attack for some time. After completing a little detour to address that attack, it is time to return to Genesis and discuss what it means for man to be created in the image and likeness of God.

There is a difference between "image" and "likeness" so we will begin with the meaning of "image" and then consider the meaning of "likeness".

---

19   Cf. Col. 3:17

Traditionally, man is said to be created in the image of God because of his powers of intellect and will, his ability to know and to choose and hence the capacity for a rational love, as compared to a purely passion driven love. That means that the image of the invisible God in the visible man is first of all found in man's invisible soul.

Further, this being in the image of God means being in the image of the Most Holy Trinity. This is hinted at in the text when God says, *Let us make man in our image, after our likeness.*[20] St. Augustine, then, instead of speaking of just intellect and will, speaks of memory, intellect, and will.

St. Thomas Aquinas develops St. Augustine's line of thought (perhaps moving more in the direction of "likeness" as we shall see) by saying that the "image" is found not so much in mere capacities of the soul, as in their action, and not just in any action, but in their action in respect to God.[21] What does that mean?

That means that while the image is rooted in the powers of the soul, it achieves its perfection, we could say, in the measure that the soul remembers God, remembering him thinks upon him, and thinking about him loves him. This reflects indeed the reality of the Most Holy Trinity in which the Father knowing himself brings forth or begets the eternal Word, his Son, and from the Father and the Son mutually knowing and loving each other the Holy Spirit proceeds as the "breath" of their mutual love.

The essential image rooted in the powers of the soul reflects the inseparable unity of the three persons, but fails to reflect their distinct personhood.

This is one reason why today it has become popular to see a sort of "image" of the Trinity in the relation of male and female, or more specifically in the relation of husband and wife.

This line of thought poses a number of difficulties and dangers. We must first avoid suggesting that the

20   Gen. 1:26
21   *ST*, Ia, q. 93

primary relation of husband and wife somehow mirrors
the relation of Father and Son in the Holy Trinity, while
the generation of the child, somehow mirrors the pro-
cession of the Holy Spirit from Father and Son, or that
the wife somehow proceeds from the husband, like the
Holy Spirit. That would be a grave error, which indeed
was one of the reasons that led St. Thomas Aquinas to
reject the comparison altogether.[22]

A better comparison, actually suggested by St. Maxi-
millian Kolbe, would see the wife and mother—after the
birth of the child—as reflecting in some way the role of
the Holy Spirit in Trinity, insofar as she helps the father
and son to know and love each other.[23]

St. Thomas Aquinas had another important objection
to the comparison of the family (husband, wife, child) to
the Trinity: namely that physical generation is common to
human beings (in the image of the Trinity) and animals
(not in the image of the Trinity).

For that reason it is very necessary to make this comparison precisely on the basis of what is characteristically
human about marriage and family. So when a man and
woman simply are joined together by passion and in this
way beget offspring, there is no particular reflection of
the Most Holy Trinity. Rather, such a reflection only
takes place when the two are joined together first by the
intelligent and intentional promise whereby they commit
their whole lives to each other, to love each other and to
beget children. Then their copulation and their begetting
of children becomes an expression of their rational love.

Further, it is through intentional and rational love that
husband and wife are not joined together only in "one
flesh" but in a true communion of persons. Consequently,
marriage and family life can only reflect the Most Holy

---

22   *ST*, Ia, q. 93, a. 6, ad. 2
23   In this case, the wife does not mirror the Holy Spirit as
proceeding from the Father, his defining personal property, but
as the "bond of love" between the Father and the Son.

Trinity in the measure that husband, wife, and children attain to a true communion of persons.

The reflection of the Trinity in the communion of the persons found in marriage and family, unlike the image in the soul, shows the reality of the union of persons, but fails to attain the unity of substance that is found within the soul. Further, we have seen that the visible reflection in marriage and family presupposes the invisible image in the soul, because the powers of intellect and will are what make true marital and family love possible.

When we begin to recognize the image in the soul, then we see that man actually transcends his activity in the created world, just as God transcends the world he created. This leads us to the sanctification of the seventh day and the Sabbath rest, which also connects to the "likeness," the reality of God's grace that brings the image to perfection through sharing in God's own knowledge and love.

SIX DAYS ARE NOT COMPLETE

God completed his work of creation after six days, but the story does not stop there. If we understand the account of creation rightly the six days will point us to the seventh day, and, in truth, creation would be incomplete without the seventh day.

Nevertheless, it is tempting to stop at the sixth day, as though the seventh day were an optional add-on. We might say that the modern world has succumbed to this temptation. We are not the first to do so.

The six days without the seventh is like the 24/7 world, a world without God. The ideology of six days, if it believes in God at all, declares that God gave the world to man to do as he pleases with it.

We see this attitude in those who would say, "It is my property. I can do with it as I please. If I choose to destroy it, that is no affair of yours."

The same attitude declares, "It is my body. I can do whatever I choose with it, even to the point of destroying the child in the womb or mutilating the sexual organs to appear as a member of the opposite sex."

This attitude has produced the degradation of the environment. The new paganism reacts to this degradation of the environment with nature worship and wrongly blames Christianity for subordinating nature to God, the Creator. I have already addressed this error. Besides being rather selective, the new paganism does not offer a real solution. The new paganism would enslave man to the caprices of nature and the caprices of human passion. The new paganism remains closed within the six days of creation.

There is perhaps an intimation of the ideology of the six days found in a famous number in the Book of Revelation. The number 666, which the Book of Revelation says is *the number of a man*, repeats the number six thrice by multiplying it tenfold and then a hundredfold.[24] Symbolically it appears as the number of man without God, man who proclaims himself as god, creation stopped on the sixth day, devoid of any purpose or meaning besides that which man himself imposes. It is the number of idolatry, whether idolatry of man or idolatry of nature.

This man-made world of idolatry is also a world without rest. Man makes himself to be a god and so must frantically rule the world he has made. This is the pattern of modern history. Man, seeking to take control of nature by the very limited means of human science and technology makes the world more complex. This in turn brings forth complex problems that were not foreseen, but which must be controlled by the same means, producing even greater complexity. It seems that the only choice is to keep up with the frantic pace of "progress" and the only solution to the ever more complex problems is more "progress." Meanwhile the world becomes increasingly inhuman and inhospitable.

Having plunged himself into this frantic world of his own making, man declares *Arbeit macht frei*—that was the

---

24   Rev. 13:18

motto over the entrance to Auschwitz; it means "work will set you free."[25] That same spirit—a demonic spirit—has given us the 24/7 world without rest and without worship. It has also given us Amazon Fulfillment Centers and the "Gig Economy."

We can well ask if we are near the point in which it will no longer be allowed to buy or sell without receiving the mark of the beast on the forehead (believing the ideology) or hand (conforming to the ideology in practice).[26]

Truly, keeping the Lord's Day holy will be key to resisting the dominion of the beast. That means, however, that we need to consider the meaning of the seventh day.

THE SEVENTH DAY

> Thus the heavens and the earth and all their array were completed. Since on the seventh day God was finished with the work he had been doing, he rested on the seventh day from all the work he had undertaken. So God blessed the seventh day and made it holy, because on it he rested from all the work he had done in creation.[27]

When we read or listen to the account of the seven days we naturally imagine God as though he were a human workman, working, laboring, and sweating for six days so that finally on the seventh day he can relax. We might then imagine him like the sculptor in his studio sitting back and admiring the statue he made seeing that it was very good.[28]

It is good to use our imagination when we read Sacred Scripture, but we must at the same time learn that our imagination is insufficient to grasp the meaning of the word of God; we need also to move beyond the imagination to the understanding of the truth that is being

---

25   Cf. Josef Pieper, *Leisure: the Basis of Culture*
26   Rev. 13:16–17
27   Gen. 2:1–3
28   Cf. Gen. 1:31

revealed by God. The words of Scripture already contain
elements that direct us beyond the imagination to the
understanding.

In the first place, we should notice that God's "work"
of creation is rather effortless. He simply commands
and it comes to be. So a "work" is produced, but without
sweat and without labor. His command meets with no
resistance.[29]

Second, we could consider some words of Jesus, by
which he justifies his performing a miracle on the Sabbath: *My Father is at work until now, and so I am at work.*[30] This
does not just refer to the work of the man Jesus Christ,
but also to the eternal activity of the Son and Word of
God. So, in the Letter to the Hebrews, we read that God
sustains all things by his mighty word.[31] In other words, through
the same Word by which God created all things in the
beginning, he continues to sustain all things in existence.[32]

So, while a human sculptor, a Michelangelo, fashions
his statue, which then continues in existence without him
and even after his death and departure from this world,
God's work only continues in existence by the same divine
power by which it was made. *In him we live, and move, and
have our being.*[33] So not only all existence, but all life and
change, and therefore all fulfillment and perfection that
comes about through change, has its origin in God. So,
the Book of Wisdom tells us that God's wisdom *reaches
from end to end mightily and governs all things well.*[34]

If, then, God is so intensely "active," so active that
the greatest of philosophers have spoken of the godhead
as "pure act" or "pure actuality," what could possibly be
meant by God's rest?

---

29 Cf. Ps. 33[32]:9
30 John 5:17
31 Heb. 1:3
32 Cf. John 1:3
33 Acts 18:28
34 Wisd. 8:1

First, we could say that God's rest tells us that his creative action does not exhaust or drain him in anyway. He creates the universe, but at the same time infinitely surpasses or "transcends" the universe he created.

When Michelangelo was actually working on a statue, every fiber of body and mind was engaged in the work, consumed in the work; the energy within him, as it were, passed into the statue; he loses something of himself in the statue. Then even when he was resting, recovering his strength, much of his waking thought would have been taken up with the project underway. When he went to Mass, or prayed, or engaged in another activity, for a time perhaps he would withdraw himself from his occupation with the statue, some part of his life and his person beyond the statue would emerge.

God, however, would be at once completely occupied with his work of creation and completely at rest in his own eternity; further, there is infinitely more to be found in God's eternity than to be found in the whole of his creation. So, God rests in himself above and beyond creation.

There is another way we could speak of God's rest. St. Augustine comments on a certain scriptural way of speaking where God will say something like "now I know" meaning "now I have made you to know." So, he stays Abraham's hand from slaying Isaac as a sacrifice, saying, *Now I know how devoted you are to God, since you did not withhold your only son from me.*[35] This means in effect that, through the trial to which he put him, God led Abraham himself to discover the depth of his own devotion to God.

If we apply this way of speaking to God's rest, then we can see that God rests on the seventh day by making his creation to rest, even more particularly by making us to rest in him.

True rest is not the mere absence of motion or change, but even more involves the attainment of a goal. So, the seventh day tells us that man was not just created for

---

35 Gen. 22:12

work in this world, however noble, but that just as God himself transcends the world, man has been created to transcend the world by resting in God. The sanctification of the seventh day, then, means the sanctification of man through which he is given to share in the holiness of God.

We can expand on this thought if we look at the seventh day precisely as the goal of the trajectory of the first six days. Biblical scholars have observed that the six days are set forth as though God were constructing a house. In the first three days, he sets up the sky as the "roof" of the house and the sea and the dry land as the two major "rooms." In the next three days, the "roof" and the "rooms" are furnished, the roof with the lights, and the rooms with the living creatures of sea, sky, and land. The principal "resident" in this house, however, is man, created in the image and likeness of God.

Now, in the ancient world, the very idea of a temple was to provide a house for an image of a "god." Seen in this way, the Genesis account of creation rejects all the pagan temples, all the temples of dead idols, because God himself constructed the whole world as a living temple in which he placed his living image.

Except in this temple of creation, the living image does not receive worship, but offers worship. Man is set in this temple not as an idol for the rest of creation to worship, but as a priest, through whom all creation can find a voice in the sacrifice of praise returned to God, the Creator. The seventh day reveals man as a priest, offering the sacrifice of praise.

There is also contained here a reflection of the Holy Trinity. Man is not exactly *the* image of God, but rather he is created *in the* image of God. The true image is the eternal Son of God, who returns to the Father in the love of the Holy Spirit. So, when God creates man in his image and man returns to God with the sacrifice of praise in the Holy Spirit, it is as though the intra-trinitarian relations are extended into the created world. In this way

seventh day represents the eternal "rest" of the Father in
the Son and of the Son in the Father; that "rest" is itself
the Holy Spirit. Through the sacrifice of praise, man is
given to share in that rest.

Nevertheless, this original creation was broken by sin.
Man turned away from his sacred task, reverted to the
sixth day, and sought to make himself the idol of the
world. The original creation was broken by sin and this
fact should warn us against any excessive glorification of
raw "nature," which is the error of much of the environmentalist movement, the religion of "Gaia," or of the
"Amazon."

In this light we can see that during the history of the
Old Testament, every true temple of God and every true
sacrifice was in some way trying to restore the broken
creation by setting apart a new "house of God," in which
there is no idol, but only a priest offering sacrifice. Temple
and sacrifice try to restore the broken creation but cannot
really do so because God does not dwell in temples built
by human hands.[36] So the temple, priesthood, and sacrifice
of the Old Testament, even more than being a reflection
of the original creation, is a figure pointing forward to
the recreation in Christ. *Therefore, a sabbath rest still remains
for the people of God. .... let us strive to enter into that rest.*[37]

The Body of Christ, crucified and risen, is the beginning
of the new creation, the new temple, not made by human
hands,[38] and also the new sacrifice, offered by the new
high priest, Jesus Christ, who offers himself upon the
Cross and continues to offer himself through the hands
of his ministers in the Holy Eucharist.

The Body of Christ, risen from the dead is the beginning of the new creation, but in the meantime the old
creation *waits with eager expectation the revelation of the children
of God; for creation was made subject to futility not of its own accord*

---

36   Cf. 1 Kings 8:27; Acts 7:47-48; 17:24
37   Heb. 4:9, 11
38   Cf. Dan. 2:34-35, 44-45; Mark 14:58; John 2:19

but because of the one who subjected it, in hope that creation itself would be set free from slavery to corruption and share in the glorious freedom of the children of God. [39]

That true freedom of the children of God is precisely the freedom to offer to God a worthy sacrifice of praise, the purpose of the whole creation. In the end when all things are made new and God is all in all, [40] in the heavenly Jerusalem, there will be no temple in the city *for its temple is the Lord God Almighty and the Lamb.* [41]

FROM THE SEVENTH DAY TO THE LORD'S DAY

I have been writing about the meaning of God's rest on the seventh day and the sanctification of the seventh day. All this leads now to a question: God commanded, *Remember to keep holy the sabbath day* .... *In six days the Lord made heaven and earth, the sea and all that is in them; but on the seventh day he rested.* [42] Why, then, do Christians observe Sunday, the first day of the week, as "the Lord's Day," and not the Sabbath, which falls on Saturday?

Actually, except for the Seventh Day Adventists, this is a big problem for Protestants, who rely on Scripture alone.

In the Gospels, we learn that Jesus rose from the dead on the first day of the week, Sunday. Apart from that there are two significant mentions of the first day of the week and one of "the Lord's Day."

In Acts we learn about St. Paul meeting with the faithful of Troas for "the breaking of the bread," probably the celebration of the Eucharist, on the first day of the week. [43]

In 1 Corinthians St. Paul writes to the Corinthians about taking up a collection for the poor of Jerusalem on the first day of the week. [44]

---

39   Rom. 8:19-21
40   Cf. Rev. 21:5; 1 Cor. 15:28
41   Rev. 21:22
42   Exod. 20:8,11
43   Acts 20:7-12
44   1 Cor. 16:2

In the book of Revelation, we learn that the seer, John, has his vision that gives rise to the book when he *was caught up in the spirit on the Lord's day.*[45]

All this tells us that the Lord's Day seems to be becoming something special in the early Church, but it hardly amounts to a clear command to observe the Lord's Day in place of the Sabbath. Indeed, when St. Paul gives the Corinthians instructions regarding the celebration of the Lord's Supper, he makes no mention of any special day of the week.[46]

Outside of Scripture, the practice of the Church quickly becomes clear. One ancient 1st century writing, the *Didache*, tells us: "Every Lord's day gather yourselves together, and break bread, and give thanksgiving after having confessed your transgressions, that your sacrifice may be pure."[47]

St. Justin Martyr, writing in about 155 AD, gave us the most ancient description of the Eucharistic celebration. He writes, "On the day we call the day of the sun, all who dwell in city or country gather in the same place."[48]

In brief, the celebration of Sunday as the Lord's Day, in place of the Sabbath, is a practice that comes to us from Sacred Tradition. Scripture bears witness to the tradition that had already begun with the Apostles, before ever any word of the New Testament was written down.[49]

Now, as for the meaning of the Lord's Day we need to recall that it is the first day of a new week.

I already observed: "The Body of Christ, crucified and risen, is the beginning of the new creation, the new temple, not made by human hands, and also the new sacrifice, offered by the new high priest, Jesus Christ, who offers himself upon the Cross and continues to offer

---

45   Rev. 1:10
46   Cf. 1 Cor. 11:17-34
47   *Didache*, 14
48   Apol, 1.67 cited in CCC 1345
49   Cf. CCC 1166

himself through the hands of his ministers in the Holy Eucharist."[50]

The original creation described in the account of the seven days, was marred by sin. It failed to achieve its purpose in the seventh day. It failed to keep God's name holy. It failed to offer him worthy sacrifice. It failed because Adam, the high priest of creation, of nature, rebelled against God.

Christ's resurrection is the beginning of a new creation, freed from sin and death. The original creation will now only achieve its purpose after Christ returns in judgment and the dead are raised, the world is transformed, and all things are made new.

Were we to continue to celebrate the Sabbath, we would be denying the work of redemption accomplished by Christ; we would be denying the resurrection; we would be denying the new creation; we would still find ourselves in the bondage of the fallen creation.

The Lord's Day, or Sunday, is the first day of the week, but it is the first day of a new week. It is the eighth day, the day of the new creation, the day of the resurrection. We no longer celebrate the first creation, but we celebrate the new creation in Christ. This is the meaning of an expression found in that ancient Christian writing already mentioned, the *Didache: "Let grace come. Let this world pass away."*[51]

On the Lord's Day, we do not just look back to Christ's resurrection from the dead, we look forward to our own bodily resurrection.

Still, with the transference of the Sabbath to the Lord's Day, we need to remember that Jesus came not to abolish the law, but to fulfill it.[52] He did this in a special way by completing the work of redemption when he died on the Cross on the sixth day, declaring, *It is finished.*[53] Then he fulfilled the Sabbath by resting in the tomb. Only then

---

50   See p. 45.
51   *Didache, 10*
52   Cf. Matt. 5:17
53   John 19:30

did he inaugurate the new creation on the eighth day, the first day of the new week.

While Jesus rested in the tomb, the light of faith in the resurrection, in the new creation, shone in the Virgin Mary. That is why now Saturday belongs in a special way to her; it is her day.

> Remember to keep holy the sabbath day. Six days you may labor and do all your work, but the seventh day is the sabbath of the Lord your God. No work may be done.... In six days the Lord made the heavens and the earth, the sea and all that is in them; but on the seventh day he rested. That is why the Lord blessed the sabbath day and made it holy.[54]

Jesus was accused of being a sabbath breaker, but he came to fulfill the law, not to abolish it. The healing work he accomplished on the sabbath was not "his" work, but his Father's work. *My Father is at work until now, so I am at work.*[55] This "work" was made necessary because the purity of the original creation was broken by Adam's sin. So, Jesus perfectly fulfilled the law of Moses first by completing the work of redemption on the sixth day, Good Friday, when he gave his life upon the Cross, saying, *It is finished.* Next he perfectly fulfilled the sabbath by resting in the tomb on the seventh day, while his Mother, the Virgin Mary, kept alive the light of faith, awaiting the dawn of the resurrection and the new creation.

Now, the sabbath has not disappeared, but it has rather been transformed in Christ; it has been moved to the first day of the week, Sunday, and has become "the Lord's Day."

If we were to be so bold as to rephrase the commandment to reflect this transformation in Christ, we would say something like:

54 Exod. 20:8-11
55 John 5:17

Remember to keep holy the Lord's Day for it is
the beginning of the new creation in Christ. On
that day you must rest in him so as to receive
new life, the life of grace, from him. Let everything that you think, do, or say proceed from
him and return to God the Father through him.
Begin the week with this rest in Christ and then
complete the work of the remaining six days,
living from the life of grace he has given you.
Complete the work of the remaining days of this
passing world with your eye always on the day
of the resurrection, the day of judgment, the day
of the new heavens and earth, when God will
make all things new.[56]

The observance of the Lord's Day is a commandment
of God that is specified by a precept of the Church, the
requirement to attend Mass on Sundays and Holy Days.
The Church makes this specification in virtue of the
authority granted her by Christ himself, *Whatever you
bind on earth will be bound in heaven.*[57]

Now, the first requirement of Christians on Sunday is
to attend Mass. This is right and just.

It is right and just because the Mass brings us into
the very heart of the Lord's Day. In the Mass we remember and proclaim the work of redemption, the work of
re-creation, in Christ, which was brought about by Jesus'
death and resurrection. Even more, that work is made
effective and operative here and now. When we are nourished by the sacrifice and sacrament of Christ's Body and
Blood, the new creation is at work in us.

To profess faith in Jesus Christ and deny the need
to attend Mass on Sunday effectively declares that we
have no need of Christ's people, the Church, and effectively denies the very faith we profess by refusing to be
re-created in him.

---

56   Cf. Rev. 21:1, 5
57   Matt. 16:19

Note, further, that in the original commandment God told the people, *six days you may labor and do your work.* That means the seventh day the people were supposed to put aside their own work, their own needs, and dedicate the day to God, to God's work.

Often we might look forward to Sunday thinking, "Now it is a day for me to do what I want." Our thinking is backwards. Sunday rather is the one day in the week, above all dedicated to God's work, to doing his will. His will is that we love God above all things and love our neighbor as ourselves for love of God. From Sunday, we carry God's will into the rest of the week.

On Sunday we practice the love of God by attending Mass, by giving extra time to prayer, and by study of the word of God and the teaching of the Church.

On Sunday we practice love of neighbor by spending time with our families, the first 'neighbors' God has put in our life, and by works of mercy in service of those in need.[58]

What about rest? It is God who will give us true rest. If on Sundays we generously give ourselves to God, we will find that he restores our energies, giving us light and strength for the week.

Contrariwise, very often when we first seek rest and relaxation, we find some physical and mental rest perhaps, but we often do so in a way that leaves us feeling empty inside. We do not return to our weekday activities with a renewed sense of purpose, but with a feeling of weariness, of being "burnt out."

When, however, we learn to put God first on Sundays, then we will learn how to find rest and relaxation that will truly restore our energies.

We should do his will at all times, but above all on Sunday. We will find our true "rest" when we rest from doing our own will and learn to do God's will.

---

58 CCC 2185

This sets up an order of priorities for Sunday: The practice of the love of God through taking part in the Mass, extra time for prayer and for study of the word of God and the teaching of the Church; the practice of love of neighbor through time spent with family and through the practice of works of mercy. All of this activity should orient us to the true rest, which will also paradoxically involve the supreme activity of the new world of the resurrection.

THE PRESENT DISORDER IN THE LIGHT OF THE LORD'S DAY

When we consider what the Lord's Day really means and what it is really for, we discover that we have a huge problem; we have a huge problem because often enough it is hard for people to get to Mass, which is but the minimum requirement for the observance of the Lord's Day.

This problem is also a kind of light, a light that reveals the grave evil and disorder of the society in which we live.

We are still in living memory of a time when most commercial activity in the United States stopped on Sunday. In many places even gas stations closed on Sundays.

Even then, there were already many encroachments. Power plants would have to continue in operation on Sundays. Many factories kept operating on Sunday because it would have been too expensive to shut down the machinery and then start it back up again on Monday. In other words, the rise of industrialism and the need for massive amounts of 'energy' introduced a new kind of necessary Sunday work.

Also, Sunday has long been dedicated more to entertainment than to worship. Some historians have written that in 19th century America rural churches, and America was mostly rural, would be filled on Sundays because the only "entertainment" available was listening to a sermon!

With the rise of sports, Sunday became a day for playing or watching baseball or football. The movie "Chariots of Fire," which is based on a true story about the British runners in the 1924 Paris Olympics, contains a dramatic scene in which one of the runners creates an uproar because he refuses to run in a race on Sunday. His refusal to run seemed rather quaint and archaic, scrupulous even, to the whole sports establishment and also the British King who accompanied the team on the boat trip across the English Channel.

In *Chariots of Fire* (1981 film) the man who stands up for the Sunday rest is a Protestant. In the 19th century, however, Our Lady of La Salette complained to the children about the peasants of the region working on Sunday.

All this took place at a time when by and large things came to a standstill on Sundays and Christian observance was still strong enough to limit the encroachments. Now, with the promotion of the social equality of all religions or none, together with the advent of the internet, whereby we are plugged in 24/7, the commercial world runs 24/7. There is no more restraint.

Further, secularization has reached the point in which our national religion of sports demands sacrifices any day (including Sunday) at any time, including for practices, with no regard for any traditional Christian observance. Parents have remained silent in the face of this onslaught because, God forbid they should deprive their children of an opportunity to participate in sports.

The Catholic Bishops of the United States, frankly, have not helped because they did not insist that allowances be made for Catholic practice, even at a time when they might have had some influence. Instead, they began dropping Holy Days altogether, or moving them to Sundays, in order not to inconvenience anyone.

Contrariwise, Jews have typically insisted strongly that allowances be made to accommodate their observances of the Sabbath and also their Holy Days. I grew up in areas where on Rosh Hashanah (the Jewish new year) half my class would be absent from school.

So we have now reached a time in which work, or sports, or even school, can effectively make demands upon us any day, any time. This reveals a disorder in society that leads to new forms of slavery.

I would actually say that Sunday observance is not just a religious issue, but a social justice issue, indeed the key issue for true social justice. Social justice means nothing if it does not involve the right order of society; if social justice is reduced to merely economic issues (or environmental issues) it completely misses the larger question of the right order of society. A rightly ordered society would put the observance of Sunday first and the good of the family second, while all work, production, and economic matters would be subordinated to these two human goods.

PART II
SOCIAL JUSTICE

FROM THE LORD'S DAY TO SOCIAL JUSTICE

Writing about creation and writing about the Lord's Day has led to a recognition that the proper Sunday observance is at the foundation of true social justice. Now it is time to pursue this line of thinking. This will mean considering the social teaching of the Church in a way that has scarcely been followed since Pope Leo XIII's foundational social encyclical *Rerum Novarum* (RN), written in 1891.

First, though, it is important to note how badly the social teaching of the Church has been received, even by Catholics.

For example, in Pope Francis' encyclical *Laudato Si'* the most important part, which really governs everything else, is his presentation of the theology of creation. People don't care much about theology; we are very practically minded. So the result has been that the theology of creation is ignored and the value of the encyclical is judged by the Pope's stance on things like climate change and the practical course of action that he suggests. In other words, the small part of the encyclical in which the Pope actually speaks within the scope of his papal teaching authority, is ignored, whereas the larger part of the encyclical, in which the Pope's voice is only one opinion among many, gets the attention.

So also, with Leo XIII's *Rerum Novarum*, many people might think of that encyclical in terms of his approval of labor unions. Few paid much attention to what he thought labor unions should be like.

Still, when Pope Leo XIII was writing in 1891 the modern process of secularization (which will necessarily involve eliminating the Lord's Day from the public life of nations) had already begun, but it was still possible for the Pope to call people to return to the Christian foundations of society. This means that the Pope is able to write more simply and directly about how things should be.

In recent decades, Catholic social teaching has been framed in the context of radically pluralistic societies and a radically pluralistic world. This has forced the Church to frame her teaching in the context of that pluralism. This has often had the unfortunate consequence (precisely because people look to the practical programs, not the underlying principles) that people begin to regard pluralism as the way things should be, as the social ideal.

If we really think about what pluralism means then we will see that it is truly an evil to be tolerated, not an ideal to be proclaimed. It must be tolerated because it cannot successfully be overcome by force.

Nevertheless, pluralism is an evil, because in the end pluralism simply means that different people have radically different underlying views of God, man, the meaning of human life, and about right and wrong. Yes, there are common elements in these different views, but those common elements take on very different meanings precisely because they are set in very different contexts.

For example, the negative form of the golden rule ("Do not to others what you would not have them do to you") is quite universal, but is also quite vague. The so-called "second table" of the Ten Commandments, those that deal with our relations with other human beings, are also fairly universal—at least before the 20th century.

Everyone accepts, "Thou shalt not kill," in some form or another. Nevertheless, the precise meaning and scope of the commandment very much depends on the underlying view of human life, which in turn depends on the underlying 'worldview'. This will in turn have an impact on how people view matters like war, capital punishment, and self-defense. The debates in these matters bear witness to underlying world views that in our practically minded world are rarely examined or discussed.

Pluralism then does not unite people but sets them in conflict. The life of a pluralistic community revolves around the question of how to manage these inevitable conflicts.

That is challenge enough when it is a matter of a pluralism of groups such as Christians, Muslims, and Jews in the Crusader Kingdoms of the Holy Land in the Middle Ages. What we have today, however, might be called the hyper-pluralism of individuals.

Even when individuals combine in larger groups, those are viewed, finally, as purely voluntary associations. In theory, at least, people are free to come and go as they please. Which means that even in religious groups the unity of worldview is more a matter of coincidence of worldviews, rather than true unity. In other words, we are together because we happen to think alike, not because there is anything real that actually unites us. That we might say is the "worldview" of pluralism.

The attempt to set forth the social teaching of the Church in this context is subject to immense challenges and readily leads to major distortions.

That makes it worthwhile to review the principles and order of an encyclical like *Rerum Novarum,* which was written before the vast civilizational destruction that took place in World War I. My intention will not be to focus so much on actual Church teaching as to reflect on the subject from the perspective of the Lord's Day. First, though, it will be good to review the foundational principles of *Rerum Novarum*.

1
Principles of Social Justice

THE FOUNDATIONAL PRINCIPLES OF LEO XIII'S
RERUM NOVARUM

As I already mentioned, during the course of the 20th century the expression of the Church's social teaching became ever more complex and convoluted as it attempted to address the situation of a society that was becoming both more complex and more secularized. *Rerum Novarum* by way of contrast stands out for the clarity of its order and principles, which will always remain foundational.

Like almost all Papal documents the title comes from the first words of the official Latin version. Here these words mean literally "Of new things" but is translated into English as "revolutionary change" and into Italian as the "craving for novelty." Traditionally "novelty" and "revolution" have not been seen as positive realities in the Catholic tradition. Novelty suggests a departure from the sacred Tradition handed down from the Apostles, while "revolution" suggests the overturning of right order and legitimate authority, which derive from God. *Let every person be subordinate to the higher authorities, for there is no authority except from God, and those that exist have been established by God.* [1]

In this case, the Pope is writing because the "spirit of revolutionary change" has passed from politics into the realm of practical economics. [2] This leads the Pope to address the Church on the condition of the working classes that have lost the protection of the ancient guilds, are threatened by the "hardheartedness of employers and the greed of unchecked competition," while the "socialists"

---

1   Rom. 13:1
2   Cf. *RN*, 1

try to exploit "the poor man's envy of the rich" in an effort to do away with all private property.[3]

The Pope's first task will be to reaffirm the right of private property. He will indeed declare: "The first and most fundamental principle, therefore, if one would alleviate the condition of the masses, must be the inviolability of private property."[4]

He then proceeds to delineate the role of the Church, which is rather extensive, because "if human society is to be healed now, in no other way can it be healed save by a return to Christian life and Christian institutions."[5]

After the consideration of the role of the Church he considers the role of the State, which will be more limited.

In all these considerations he speaks of different aspects of the relation between employers and workers, but only at the very end does he speak directly about what employers and workers can themselves do. "In the last place, employers and workmen may of themselves effect much, in the matter We are treating, by means of associations and organizations."[6] It is in this context that he will finally talk about "workingmen's unions."

Now let's take a look at some of the particulars of the Pope's teaching.

He rejects the socialist attempt to eliminate private property, moving everything into the realm of the State. He points out that the working man himself would be among the first to suffer, and that the elimination of private property would be "emphatically unjust, for it would rob the lawful possessor, distort the functions of the State, and create utter confusion in the community."[7]

The Pope then proceeds to explain the purpose and right of property starting first from the nature of man and then from the nature of the family.

3   *RN*, 2–4
4   *RN*, 15
5   *RN*, 27
6   *RN*, 49
7   *RN*, 4

A man engages in work for wages, which are at his disposal, through which he desires to acquire some sort of permanent property, and so better the material conditions of his life.[8] More important, by his power of reason, a man has the capacity to provide for his future needs, and property is one of the chief means of doing so.[9] Further, by the very labor that a man employs to work the land or fashion some object that is useful or beautiful, he transforms the raw materials, making them his own.[10] Consequently, even though God has given the earth for the good of the whole human race, this does not bar the owning of property because it has not been given to all without distinction "but rather no part of it has been assigned to any one in particular, and the limits of private possession have been left to be fixed by man's own industry, and by the laws of individual races."[11]

Even more important, in relation to private property, is the divine institution of marriage and family, the first and most fundamental human society, that is older than any State, and "and has rights and duties peculiar to itself which are quite independent of any State."[12]

What the Pope affirms about marriage and family here is of paramount importance for Catholic social teaching. All too often social justice is viewed purely in terms of the relations among individuals and between individuals and the State. Nevertheless, by nature the family stands between the individual and the State. An individual always belongs to a family, before he belongs to a State.

When we read what Pope Leo XIII writes here it goes quite contrary to what have become the underlying principles of our contemporary culture. I would say it is our contemporary culture that is wrong, not Pope Leo XIII.

---

8   Cf. *RN*, 5
9   Cf. *RN*, 6–7
10 Cf. *RN*, 9–10
11 *RN*, 8
12 *RN*, 12

In what follows, it is important to realize that if Pope
Leo XIII is right, then it lays bare the depth and extent
of our present social disorder but does not exactly show
us how to right the situation. Likewise, in my own comments on the Pope's teaching, if I criticize any present
reality, my intent is not to say, "Go out and change it right
now." Still, if we gain some glimpse of right order, then
it makes sense that we move in that direction, the best
we can, given our actual circumstances and limitations.

The Pope writes:

> It is a most sacred law of nature that a father
> should provide food and all necessaries for those
> whom he has begotten; and, similarly, it is nat-
> ural that he should wish that his children who
> carry on, so to speak, and continue his personality,
> should be provided by him with all that is need-
> ful to enable them to keep themselves decently
> from want and misery amid the uncertainties
> of this mortal life. Now, in no other way can
> a father effect this except by the ownership of
> productive property, which he can transmit to
> his children by inheritance. A family, no less
> than a State, is, as We have said, a true soci-
> ety, governed by an authority peculiar to itself,
> that is to say, by the authority of the father.....
> Paternal authority can be neither abolished nor
> absorbed by the State; for it has the same source
> as human life itself.[13]

Today we have become so dominated by feminist thinking, with its rejection of any special paternal authority,
that we have come to take its principles for granted.[14]

---

13   *RN,* 13, 14
14   While there are many "feminisms" I generally speak of "feminism" in terms of what I grew up with, and was surrounded by,
as a dominant cultural influence already through the 70s. This
has set the terms of public discussion such that "patriarchy" has
become a dirty word, such that men are regarded as unqualified to

Feminist thinking, however, fundamentally rejects the family as the keystone of human social life and builds everything on the isolated individual. Feminist thinking is built on the presupposition that we are all, by nature, equal and distinct individuals, who have the right to advance ourselves and fashion our lives as we wish. On this view sexual differences are wholly secondary and quite irrelevant. Family remains an option that some might choose, if they wish, but what becomes primary is the pursuit of a job and career path that will serve individual fulfillment. Men and women are seen as having completely equal rights and capacity in this matter and family roles must take second place.

This way of thinking, as widespread as it has become, is quite arbitrary, artificial, and against nature. It is we could say destructive of the fundamental structure of human "ecology," the family. In the end it reduces human beings to being nothing more than interchangeable cogs in the vast machinery of production.

The difference between male and female remains an irreducible fact of human life, but, as Pope Francis has often observed, we no longer know how to treat of the difference. This has produced immense confusion and arising from the confusion untold personal damage. Finally, we can only find our identity, our purpose, and our fulfillment in life through our masculinity and femininity. Not as undifferentiated "humans."

In stark contrast to modern feminism, the teaching of Pope Leo XIII is openly patriarchal. "Patriarchy" should

---

address the subject, unless it is to support feminism. The protest is a symptom of a disorder, about which I will have something to say, but the cure has been worse than the disease. Women, because of their ability to become pregnant and their physical weakness (generally speaking) in relation to men have certain unique vulnerabilities that will always be there. Those vulnerabilities are best protected by good men in a well-ordered society. The other choice is government, which will not be good government; this option also has a way of making good men ever harder to find.

not be a dirty word. It really speaks to the fundamental principle of all rightly ordered human social life. If the authority of the father is rejected, as it has been today, there can be no true social justice.

The claim, which in the time of Pope Leo XIII would have been fairly uncontroversial, at least among Catholics, might seem intolerably extreme today, even among Catholics.

If we are going to speak in a positive way of patriarchy, then it is absolutely essential to distinguish authority from raw power.

Power, we could say, is simply the ability to act, whether for good or ill. Authority, however, is power that is ordered and legitimized through hierarchical subordination that has its ultimate source in God, the ruler of all, the supreme authority, whose power is always exercised with wisdom and justice. Authority, then, when it is possessed by intelligent creatures, is always received from a higher authority, always limited in its scope by that higher authority, and always accountable to that higher authority, always answerable to God, the supreme authority. When, one possessing authority exercises power beyond the scope of his authority, it becomes an abuse of power, lacks authority, and cannot bind the conscience of his subjects. In the end, the subject must always obey the higher authority, rather than submit to the abuse of power by the lower authority; it is necessary to obey God, not man.[15]

Pope Leo XIII effectively affirms that the authority of the father in the family is the fundamental principle of right social order. It is necessary now to clarify a bit what that does and does not mean.

It is one thing to uphold the authority of the father, in principle, but another to discover the best way of proceeding when, in particular cases, a father becomes abusive or tyrannical. Likewise, upholding the authority of the father, in principle, does not exclude particular cases in

15   Acts 5:29

which, for example, a mother has to step in because of the incapacity or absence of the father. These matters involve adaptation, in particular circumstances, because of a wound, even a grievous wound. This adaptation is easier and more possible when the larger social order is healthy and supportive; it is ultimately made possible because at the root of all social order is God, the Father and Ruler of all.

It is one thing to adapt the application of paternal authority in particular circumstances, but it is another thing to reject the very principle of paternal authority altogether, as does feminism and the actual feminist legal system.

Ironically, one of the feminist arguments in favor of abortion is a "right to privacy" which holds that the government should not enter the intimacy of the bedroom. Nevertheless, the feminist rejection of paternal authority required radical government intervention into the very structure of family life. More and more, the family becomes a mere creature of the State, allowed and tolerated only insofar as the State permits. Feminism, in fact, has chosen to make women dependent on an impersonal bureaucratic State, rather than on a husband. That was the message of the 2012 Obama Campaign's "Life of Julia" informercial, in which no man appeared and the government had taken over the traditional roles first of father, then of husband.

The authority of the father establishes the family as an ordered society. It is not a matter of better or worse, superior or inferior, but, as we like to say these days, it is a matter of complementarity. We could put the matter this way: it belongs to the husband and father to build the house, either literally or through his work; only the wife and mother can make the house to be a home. That also means that the man normally should be the leader in the public realm outside of the home, but inside the woman is the queen.

Pope Pius XI wrote:

> Domestic society being confirmed, therefore, by
> this bond of love, there should flourish in it that
> "order of love," as St. Augustine calls it. This
> order includes both the primacy of the husband
> with regard to the wife and children, the ready
> subjection of the wife and her willing obedience,
> which the Apostle commends ... This subjection,
> however, does not deny or take away the liberty
> which fully belongs to the woman both in view
> of her dignity as a human person, and in view
> of her most noble office as wife and mother and
> companion; nor does it bid her obey her hus-
> band's every request if not in harmony with right
> reason or with the dignity due to wife; nor, in
> fine, does it imply that the wife should be put on
> a level with those persons who in law are called
> minors, to whom it is not customary to allow
> free exercise of their rights on account of their
> lack of mature judgment, or of their ignorance
> of human affairs. But it forbids that exaggerated
> liberty which cares not for the good of the family;
> it forbids that in this body which is the family,
> the heart be separated from the head to the great
> detriment of the whole body and the proximate
> danger of ruin. For if the man is the head, the
> woman is the heart, and as he occupies the chief
> place in ruling, so she may and ought to claim
> for herself the chief place in love.[16]

Our homes in this world are but temporary, but, if
we are left homeless from our birth, we are poor and
miserable, no matter what else we have.

When we see people living out on the street and call
them "homeless" and when we speak about the lack of
housing and the crisis of homelessness, we are actually
seeing only a small part of the picture. There are an

16   *Castii Conubii,* 26–27

increasing number of people who, even though they live
in houses or apartments, really have no idea any longer
what a 'home' really is. Very often people loosely related,
maybe even a true family, live in a house where they sleep,
but scarcely spend any other time there, while each goes
his separate way during the day.

So, while recognizing the present economic reality
that can make it very difficult for a woman to dedicate
herself to fashioning a real home, perhaps it is time for
married couples to find ways for the wife to spend time
fulfilling her unique maternal homemaking role. It would
help also if we begin to show real esteem for motherhood
and the maternal gift of woman, if we stop teaching little
girls that real "success" comes in pursuing a career, and
if we stop glorifying examples of career women as "what
a woman can be and do."

After talking about the importance of the family and
the necessity of property for family life, the Pope then
speaks of the necessity of the Church in the matter of
social justice, boldly declaring: *no practical solution of this
question will be found apart from the intervention of religion and
the Church.*[17]

The Church has (or had) numerous institutions that
organize men in the service of human needs, organizations
that operate not by means of the coercive power of the
State but impelled by the love of Christ.[18]

The Church also guides human life by means of her
divine teaching that not only makes clear to all the natural law, but also reminds mankind of the need to bear
the pains and hardships that are part and parcel of our
earthly life. The Church also teaches the true meaning
of the various social and economic inequalities that will
always be present in life, but rather than setting men in
the opposition of class conflict, reminds both the rich
and the working class of their mutual duties towards each

17 *RN*, 16
18 Cf. 2 Cor. 5:14

other and the precept of true charity that should "bind class to class in friendliness and good feeling."[19]

This also makes clear the distinction between the mere possession of private property and its proper use. The Pope quotes St. Thomas Aquinas: "Man should not consider his material possessions his own, but as common to all, so as to share them without hesitation when others are in need."[20]

Yet, the Church's teaching keeps the mutual relations of the rich and the working class, the employer and employed, from degenerating into a merely contractual exchange of goods, labor for work done, in which the employer is quit of his obligations at 5pm and when the paycheck is signed. He writes:

> Justice demands that, in dealing with the working man, religion and the good of his soul must be kept in mind. Hence the employer is bound to see that the worker has time for his religious duties; that he not be exposed to corrupting influences and dangerous occasions; and that he be led not away to neglect his home and family, or to squander his earnings. Further, the employer must never tax his work people beyond their strength or employ them in work unsuited to their sex and age.[21]

Absolutely key is the teaching that "the things of earth cannot be understood or valued aright without taking into consideration the life to come, the life that will know no death."[22] In this light we come to understand that Christ did not take away the pains and sorrows that are woven together with our mortal life, but "transformed them into motives of virtue and occasions of merit."[23] Indeed, "No man can hope for eternal reward unless he follow

---

19   *RN*, 21
20   *RN*, 22
21   *RN*, 20
22   *RN*, 21
23   Ibid.

in the blood-stained footprints of the Savior."[24] In the same light the rich learn that their riches are of no avail for eternal happiness, while those who lack "the goods of fortune" are "taught by the Church that in God's sight poverty is no disgrace, and that there is nothing to be ashamed of in earning their bread by labor."[25] So, finally,

> if Christian precepts prevail, the respective classes will not only be united in the bonds of friendship, but also in those of brotherly love. For they will understand and feel that all men are children of the same common Father, who is God; that all have alike the same last end, which is God himself, who alone can make men or angels absolutely and perfectly happy; that each and all are redeemed and made sons of God, by Jesus Christ.[26]

Even more, the Church, does not only teach and guide men, "she possesses a power peculiarly her own."[27] Though he does not name them, he refers here to the sacraments, by which God pours his grace into the hearts of men. So he continues:

> The instruments which she employs are given to her by Jesus Christ himself for the very purpose of reaching the hearts of men, and derive their efficiency from God. They alone can reach the innermost heart and conscience, and bring men to act from a motive of duty, to control their passions and appetites, to love God and their fellow men with a love that is outstanding and of the highest degree and to break down courageously every barrier which blocks the way to virtue.[28]

---

24   Ibid.
25   *RN*, 23
26   *RN*, 25
27   *RN*, 26
28   Ibid.

The Church in many ways cares for the temporal needs of men, seeking to help "the poor" to "rise above poverty and wretchedness and better their condition of life". Nevertheless, it is precisely by following the law of Christ and practicing virtue, while treading the road to eternal life, that the material condition of man is most truly helped, both because this way of life wins the blessing of God, and because of the good order of the virtuous life itself.[29]

In sum, the Church is necessary for the right order of human society by means of her benevolent institutions, her divine teaching, and above all the sacraments of grace that make a life of goodness, justice, and holiness truly possible.

Finally, we must turn our attention to the State. Nevertheless, I will not enter too much into what Pope Leo XIII has to say about the State. The reason is that the Pope's teaching here refers to "the State as rightly apprehended ... any government conformable in its institutions to right reason and natural law."[30] I don't know that there exists such a government in the world today. Here again, the current expression of the Church's social teaching has become rather contorted by the attempt to address a radically distorted situation, while this contortion is readily mistaken for the ideal situation.

The Pope makes reference to an earlier encyclical he had written "On the Christian Constitution of the State" (*Immortale Dei*) in which he teaches that man is obliged to offer right worship to God, not just individually, but socially and publicly. As a result he teaches:

> It is a sin for the State not to have care for
> religion as something beyond its scope, or as
> of no practical benefit; or out of many forms
> of religion to adopt that one which chimes in
> with the fancy; for we are bound absolutely to

---

29   *RN*, 28
30   *RN*, 32

worship God in that way which He has shown
to be His will. All who rule, therefore, would
hold in honour the holy name of God, and one
of their chief duties must be to favour religion,
to protect it, to shield it under the credit and
sanction of the laws, and neither to organize
nor enact any measure that may compromise
its safety.[31]

In other words, right social order today gets off on
the wrong foot by denying the foundational role of the
father in the family and the foundational role of religion
in the State. Instead, the State, dismisses religion as an
unimportant merely private matter, while it tends to take
over the whole of human life. The State, recognizing
no "upward" limit as regards religion and no "downward"
limit in the family, tends towards totalitarianism, even if
it be the soft totalitarianism of modern democracy about
which Alexis de Tocqueville warned.[32] Where the State
does not acknowledge God, the State tends to substitute
itself in the place of God. Where Caesar does not render
God his due, he claims all as due to himself.

So consider what Pope Leo XIII writes about the State
in *Rerum Novarum*:

A State chiefly prospers and thrives through
moral rule, well-regulated family life, respect
for religion and justice, the moderation and fair
imposing of public taxes, the progress of arts and
of trade, the abundant yield of the land—through
everything, in fact, which makes the citizens
better and happier.[33]

Today, however, the political, economic, and social order,
instead of being built around the right worship of God and
the protection of the family hearth and home, is directed

31   *Immortale Dei*, 6
32   Cf. *Democracy in America*
33   *RN*, 32

to the extension of material prosperity to more and more
individuals (at least that is the ideal). This order of individual material prosperity requires a massive bureaucratic
State so as better to achieve the goal without in any way
requiring that people actually be good, just, or virtuous.
Quite the contrary, the current order of things forms
people to be consumers of products, produced by machines.
It is an order not of persons, but of machines, delivering
products to consumers. On one side, man, as worker, is
just a cog in the vast machinery; on the other side, man,
as consumer, is the supposed beneficiary of the machinery.

Unfortunately, the Church today, while she has raised
her voice against materialism and consumerism, and while
she has raised her voice to protest in favor of those who
end up cast aside and discarded by the machinery of
production, has in practice yielded to the secularization
of society, which is inherently atheistic and anti-family,
and the root of the whole current disorder.

THE ORDER OF EDEN AND ITS LOSS

I began writing about the truth of creation and the
limitations of modern science. My consideration of creation finished with the sabbath and the Lord's Day. This
led me to affirm that the Lord's day is actually the most
important institution of true social justice.

I wrote:

> Social justice means nothing if it does not involve
> the right order of society; if social justice is
> reduced to merely economic issues (or environ-
> mental issues) it completely misses the larger
> question of the right order of society. A rightly
> ordered society would put the observance of Sun-
> day first and the good of the family second, while
> all work, production, and economic matters would
> be subordinated to these two human goods.[34]

---

34   See p. 54.

Before beginning to look at this order of social justice, starting from the Lord's Day, I turned first to some foundational principles of the Church's social teaching, as enunciated by Pope Leo XIII in *Rerum Novarum*. There we saw how in dealing with the issues of private property and the relation between employer and worker, he taught that these issues do not revolve around just the well-being of individuals, but the well-being of the family, which is the first and foundational human society. We also saw that he was insistent on the necessary role of religion and the Church for the right order of human society.

Pope Leo XIII, as well as his successors, have approached the matter addressing particular problems agitating the society of their times. Pope Leo XIII was particularly concerned to defend the right of private property over against socialism and communism. Later, in the 20th century, after World War II, complicated issues involving global economic disparity between developed and undeveloped nations, which were further exacerbated by the conflics of the Cold War, entered into the picture. More recently, environmental issues have been given a great deal of attention. In the end, the pressure of immediate practical concerns in a highly secularized world, have tended to obscure the very foundations of social order, foundations that have been so eroded as to seem no longer relevant to actual life.

My argument is that it is necessary to renew our understanding of the foundations, even if they have been practically destroyed, because we will never get it right unless those foundations are restored. Such a goal might seem remote and impractical, but the vision of the goal reveals the depth of corruption of our actual social, economic, and political order. Without the vision of how things should be we will only be swept along further by the tide of corruption. Further, the vision of right order is needed so that individuals, families, and smaller communities can begin coalescing around such sound principles, providing the seeds and foundation for future renewal. Compromises and half-measures will get us nowhere. If nothing else, we must at least keep the vision alive.

That is what the Jewish people, in captivity in Babylon did, when they sang, *If I forget you, Jerusalem, let my right-hand wither.*[35]

So let's begin with the original order, the order of Eden.

When Adam and Eve were first created they enjoyed the grace and friendship of God, their Creator. They possessed such perfect innocence, interior order in their souls, and dominion over their bodies, that they could live in each other's presence, in the complete transparency of their nakedness, without any shame or need for shame. Finally, they lived in perfect harmony with the created world, over which they had been given dominion under God.

In sum, in Eden, there was perfection and peace in four hierarchical orders: the order of man to God, the interior order of the individual human person, the social order that begins in the relation of male and female, and finally the order of man over the whole creation.[36]

St. Augustine defined peace as "the tranquility of order"; in Eden, before sin, there was perfect peace because there was perfect order.

Notice what happens next. First, Adam and Eve disobey the divine commandment, thereby breaking their right relation to God, disrupting the first and most fundamental order, losing thereby the grace and friendship of God.

Next, everything else falls into disorder.

They see that they are naked. In other words, they have been stripped of the clothing of divine grace, they have lost their own personal innocence, the right order of their soul, and dominion of soul over body. Hence, they have become weak, vulnerable, and ashamed.

From this comes the disruption of their mutual relation as they cover their shame, hide from each other, and

---

35 Ps. 137[136]:5
36 Cf. CCC 374–379

enter into the bitterness of mutual recrimination that has haunted human life ever since.

Finally, their relation with the created world over which they were meant to exercise a benevolent dominion, was disrupted as they were cast out of the garden and had to toil and sweat to gain their bread from the midst of thorns and thistles.

In all this disorder resulting from sin, the relation to God and the interior order of the human soul is key.

This means that unless the right relationship with God is restored, every other order within the created world, is doomed to failure.

The word "religion" means, by its etymology, "binding back." The practice of religion is what is meant to "bind us back" to God, and so restore that first and most fundamental order.

In this, however, not all religions are equal, but only that religion that is willed by God will do.

NATURAL LAW IS NOT ENOUGH

Note, that I have taken as my starting point what God has revealed to us through his word in sacred Scripture. This is a "theological" starting point that is not altogether accessible to unaided human reason. The contemporary Catholic approach to social justice in a pluralistic society has sought to appeal instead to the "natural law" as a philosophical starting point, accessible in theory to all, believer and non-believer alike.

This is first of all seen as a practical necessity because of the separation between Church and State and because society must include believers of different sorts, as well as non-believers. From this, because an individual must freely embrace the faith and cannot be coerced in this regard, founding human society on natural law seems to be more than a practical necessity, but the true ideal that would allow individuals freely to discover and embrace right religion.

We need, then, to consider briefly what "natural law" is all about and whether it can truly be a sufficient foundation for human society.

St. Thomas Aquinas defines the natural law as the participation of the rational creature in the eternal law, while the eternal law is nothing other than the plan of divine providence by which he governs the universe.[37] At first glance, though, this definition appears to be "theological" because it starts with God and his providential governance of the universe.

If we were to consider natural law from a human perspective, we would say that it is the law that human reason is able to perceive as being "written" so to speak in human nature itself.

A wolf acts in determinate ways by the instinct of its own nature. We could say that the "law'" of the wolf is simply those patterns of behavior that are characteristic of wolf life. The wolf does not, however, recognize and understand this "law" and choose to obey or disobey. It simply acts according to its nature. So it is with the rest of animate and inanimate creation.

Man, however, precisely because he possesses a rational nature, is capable of understanding his own nature and the goods proper to his nature. In this way he is also capable of discerning a "law" by which he *should* act in conformity with his nature so as to attain the true human good. He is also capable of choosing not to act in conformity with his nature or of acting against his nature.

St. Thomas roots the whole of natural law in certain fundamental human goods: the good of human life itself, the good of procreation and education of children, and the goods of truth, friendship, and human society.[38]

Rightly considered the very concept of a "wolf nature" or a "human nature" intelligible to the human mind implies the existence of an intelligent Creator who designed those

37   *ST*, Ia-IIae, q. 91, a. 1–2
38   *ST*, Ia-IIae, q. 94, a. 2

natures, endowing them with their properties and characteristics. For this reason all forms of atheism end up denying the reality of human nature as a "given" that would determine some sort of "law" for man. Others might accept the reality of human nature but would deny that it can impose any sort of law or moral obligation on individuals. They say that you can't argue from an "is" to an "ought." Atheism is at least implicit in this line of thought as well.

We see here then the inability of natural law to establish a common foundation for human society between those who recognize the existence of God and atheists who deny the existence of God. Really, the only sort of morality that an atheist, if he is consistent, ends up accepting is a morality of pragmatism or utilitarianism. He will accept that in general people should do what is beneficial or useful for the greatest number, but this will vary according to circumstances. Further, when push comes to shove, the atheist will have little reason to prioritize what is beneficial or useful to the greatest number over what might be beneficial or useful for himself.

We can see, then, that the natural law really proves to be an insufficient foundation for human social life, so long as atheism is a substantial force in human society. Atheists claim to build their life on human reason, but they do not accept the natural law as belonging to the realm of reason.

That is why, in the end, the proposal to outlaw abortion or to define marriage as being between one man and one woman have been rejected in American society as impositions of religious belief.

Natural law is also insufficient as a basis for community among adherents of different religions. To put the matter simply, not all religions equally accept the force of human reason. For example, wide swaths of Islam actually reject the validity of human reason.

Indeed, today we are in many ways caught between a militant Islam that rejects reason altogether and various forms of "scientific atheism" that exalt the authority of reason over all, but at the same time truncate reason, reducing its scope to the realm of empirical facts, while removing from the realm of reason the entire realm of God and morality.

Nevertheless, even were natural law accepted as the basis for community by diverse groups and diverse religions, it would still be insufficient.

The good of truth requires that the existence of God be recognized and that the person of God be duly honored, both individually and socially. In other words, natural law is not neutral in the matter of religion but demands that God be worshipped.

In some measure the 3rd commandment, *Keep holy the Sabbath*, belongs to the natural law, but only insofar as it is reasonable to set aside determinate times for the worship of God.[39] God's commandment, however, goes beyond the generality of natural law and determines that one particular day be set aside and dedicated to the worship of God. God's commandment also determines specific rituals that are beyond the scope of natural law as such.

Indeed, because God does make known that he wants to be worshipped in a specific way, it is now against the divine law to worship him in another way. Suppose a group of Muslims, Jews, and Christians made a common agreement to worship God together so as to live in peace with each other and determined on certain prayers or rites of worship that were not specific to any of their religions. If they began offering worship to God according to those prayers or rites, it would be contrary to the worship established by God and offensive to him.

The Church has condemned Freemasonry partly because, at best, it proclaims a purely natural religion of "reason" that transcends the differences between the ancient religions.

---

39   *ST*, Ia-IIae, q. 100, a. 1

One might wonder if the new "Abrahamic Family House" in Abu Dhabi, with its mosque, synagogue, and church, all built on a common foundation, does not contain a similar misguided effort to find a unity other than the unity that God himself gives.

If religion were no more than a matter of man reaching out towards God, this might make sense, but once God has revealed himself to man in the Word through whom he made all things, there can be no human unity apart from that revelation. This is even implicit in Vatican II's formulation that the Catholic Church "is in Christ like a sacrament or as a sign and instrument both of a very closely knit union with God and of the unity of the whole human race."[40]

There is, finally, one other reason for the insufficiency of the natural law: human ignorance and weakness. Without the help of divine revelation human reason itself has difficulty grasping the natural law in its fulness. Further, the will unaided by grace readily goes astray from the good that is known when this conflicts with personal desire and interest. Then, when the will goes astray, the mind readily finds excuses, rationalizations, which plunge the mind even further into darkness. Much of moral debate in our society today has more to do with self-justification than with right and wrong.

Right religion is needed to give light to the mind and strength to the will. Without that light and strength human social life ends in conflict and corruption.

There is a further problem here: the attempt to found human society on natural law limits the vision of the human good to this passing world because the natural law is incapable of seeing past death. Nor will it do to practice religion merely for the sake of the well-being of the temporal community or nation. This turns religion upside down.

---

40 *Lumen Gentium, 1*

Worship must be offered to God because he is God and for the sake of the good that he provides for us, which above all is the good of eternal life in himself. The temporal order, governed by natural law, cannot stand on its own. Temporal society needs to be ordered to eternity, but it cannot be so ordered without right religion. Indeed, temporal society cannot be ordered to eternity except through the Lord's Day.

THE ORDER OF THE MASS:
THE FOUNDATION OF ALL RIGHT ORDER

I have been writing about the principles of social justice. Social justice means nothing if it does not mean the right order of human society. We see the foundational principles of that order in Eden where there is right order of man to God, right order in the human soul, right order between man and woman, the fundamental human society, and right order of man over creation. That order was disrupted when man rebelled against God and can only be restored in the measure that man first returns to God through right religion. Because the modern world is practically founded on the rejection of right religion all its attempts to restore the right order of human society will be vain and useless. *Unless the Lord builds the house in vain do the builders labor.*[41]

Further, I have shown that the natural law, by itself, is insufficient to restore the right order of man to God; a merely natural religion is actually offensive to God. The temporal order of human society needs not only to be ordered to God, but also to the divinely willed, supernatural goal of man and all creation, eternal life and the heavenly Jerusalem. The fundamental principle of this order is the Lord's Day, which celebrates the beginning of the new creation in the resurrection of Jesus Christ and the inbreaking of his grace and salvation into this world of time. The principle activity of the Lord's Day is the celebration of

41   Ps. 127[126]:1

the Holy Sacrifice of the Mass, which is the sacrifice of our reconciliation and salvation, the renewal of the new and eternal covenant in the Blood of Christ, the worship in spirit and truth that the Father desires, the only worship that is truly worthy of God and pleasing to him. The order of the Mass is the foundation of all right order.[42]

That means that when disorder enters the order of the Mass, as has taken place since Vatican II on account of widespread liturgical abuse, the whole order of society is threatened.[43] Ironically, many "social justice" Masses, in

---

42   One might think that Vatican II dispensed with all this, but in the new liturgy, in the Preface II of the Holy Eucharist, which is used on Corpus Christi, there is a remarkably strong expression: "At the Last Supper with his Apostles, establishing the saving memorial of the Cross, he offered himself to you as the unblemished Lamb, the acceptable gift of perfect praise. Nourishing your faithful by this sacred mystery, you make them holy so that the whole human race, bounded by one world, *may be enlightened by one faith, and united by one bond of charity*" (emphasis added). If enlightened by one faith and united by one bond of charity, then they must also be joined in a common act of worship, the offering of the unblemished Lamb, the acceptable gift of perfect praise.

43   Pope Benedict XVI affirmed that the actual reform of the Missal was not what the Council Fathers asked for, did not develop organically from the already existing Missal, and that the suppression of the earlier Missal was not right. (cf. Letter to Prof. Wolfgang Waldstein, 1976) While he accepted the new Missal as licit and legitimate, that it brought with it certain improvements and enrichments, he thought that the break with and suppression of the earlier Missal had introduced a wound in the heart of the Church. He was adamant that his Motu Proprio "Summorum Pontificum," which restored the right of citizenship, so to speak, to the old Missal, was not merely a concession to the Society of St. Pius X. (cf. *Last Testament*, 2016) Rather, it was needed to heal the wound: "What earlier generations held as sacred, remains sacred and great for us too, and it cannot be all of a sudden entirely forbidden or even considered harmful. It behooves all of us to preserve the riches which have developed in the Church's faith and prayer, and to give them their proper place." (Letter to Bishops accompanying Motu Proprio Summorum Pontificum) If the order of the Mass is the foundation of all right order, then this wound that Pope Benedict XVI sought to heal has ramifications far beyond the ceremonial of the Church.

which the Mass has been placed at the service of motivating some form of "social justice" activism, by undermining the order of the Mass have actually worked against true social justice.

The right order of things is expressed in this beautiful, but neglected, passage from the Council:

> The liturgy, "through which the work of our redemption is accomplished," most of all in the divine sacrifice of the Eucharist, is the outstanding means whereby the faithful may express in their lives, and manifest to others, the mystery of Christ and the real nature of the true Church. It is of the essence of the Church that she be both human and divine, visible and yet invisibly equipped, eager to act and yet intent on contemplation, present in this world and yet not at home in it; and she is all these things in such wise that in her the human is directed and subordinated to the divine, the visible likewise to the invisible, action to contemplation, and this present world to that city yet to come, which we seek. While the liturgy daily builds up those who are within into a holy temple of the Lord, into a dwelling place for God in the Spirit, to the mature measure of the fullness of Christ, at the same time it marvelously strengthens their power to preach Christ, and thus shows forth the Church to those who are outside as a sign lifted up among the nations under which the scattered children of God may be gathered together, until there is one sheepfold and one shepherd.44

Observe the fundamental order: human subordinate to divine, visible to invisible, action to contemplation, present world to the city yet to come.

We can consider, in miniature, the order that is produced by the Mass, if we consider the life of a contemplative

44 *Sacrosanctum Concilium, 2*

Benedictine monastery, meant to be a "school of the Lord's service," in which nothing is to be set before the "work of God," the sacrifice of praise.[45]

Fr. Hugh Somerville-Knapman of the Douai Abbey wrote:

> Monks live liturgy. "Let nothing be preferred to the Work of God" our holy father St Benedict bids us. The Divine Office and the Mass punctuate and structure our day, uniting our lives with Christ's sacrifice of perfect praise in his Body and Blood on the Cross. This union is what gives the monk's life its truest and deepest value.[46]

I had the privilege of residing for about 9 months at the Abbey of Notre Dame de Fontgombault in France. The monastery was originally founded in 1091 but was suppressed in 1791 during the time of the French Revolution. It was refounded in 1948 as a daughter house of St. Peter of Solesmes. The Abbey of Fontgombault has since established other monasteries (daughter houses) including one in Clear Creek, Oklahoma.

I have a vivid memory of standing in the ancient Romanesque Abbey church as the bells for Lauds were ringing and watching the monks process in to chant the praises of God, just as they had done for centuries, apart from the interruption of about 150 years that was a result of a rebellion against God.

The monks live for God and for eternity, not for this world. Their day is structured around the fixed hours of prayer. At Fontgombault, the conventual Mass followed the hour of Terce, chanted at 10am. The priests would also each celebrate private Masses early in the morning. Everything is built on the Holy Sacrifice, everything is ordered to the Holy Sacrifice, everything flows from the

---

45   Cf. *Rule of St. Benedict*, Prologue, Ch. 43
46   Cited at https://vultuschristi.org/index.php/2014/02/let-nothing
-be-preferred-to-the-work-of-god/

Holy Sacrifice. Surrounding the Holy Sacrifice as a crown, or as the setting of the jewel, are the hours of the Divine Office, sanctifying the times of the day. There is the office of Vigils (in the wee hours of the morning), Lauds, Prime (the first hour), Terce, Sext, None, Vespers, and Compline.

The well-known rhythm of Benedictine life is "Ora et Labora," pray and work. All activity outside the hours of Mass and the Divine Office has to fit into the schedule of prayer. Preparation of meals, work in the garden, or the vineyard, or the forest, cleaning, laundry, maintenance work, as well as the study and teaching that is part of the monastic life, are all structured around the hours of prayer.

So also community recreation. On a few occasions I had the privilege of joining the monastic community for their "recreation" when they sat together and chatted. The conversation was lively, but when the bell rang for office it was as though someone turned off the volume.

That is the Rule of St. Benedict: "Let nothing be preferred to the Work of God."[47]

The monastery, according to St. Benedict, is to be a school of the Lord's service so everything in the life is structured that the monks might remember God continually, do his will, and give him praise.[48]

Because everything is structured around the hours of prayer all the other activities, from cleaning bathrooms, to plowing fields, to cooking, to studying philosophy and theology, sustain, in one way or another, the common life of the monks, the community of divine praise, and are thereby taken up into the life of praise and ennobled thereby.

When a monk who is cleaning a bathroom hears the bell ring for prayer, lays down his scrub brush, washes his hands, and goes to the church to join the song of praise, the scrub brush, the toilet, and the sweat of his brow, all rise up to God with that chorus of praise. When he returns to the bathroom 15 minutes later, he returns,

---

47   *Rule*, Ch. 43
48   Cf. Prologue to the Rule

we could say, with the light and love of God to fill and transform his humble work of service.

In the monastery we see clearly the ultimate purpose of all human activity in this world, from the simplest and most mundane to the most elevated and sophisticated.

All the prayer and work of the monks is also characterized by gratuitousness. The monks are all there because they have freely chosen to be there, they have freely consecrated themselves, their whole lives to the service of God in the monastery. Their gift of themselves in the monastic vows is itself a response to the recognition of God's gift, the gift of creation, the gift of redemption, the gift of grace. Everything in life, in the order of nature and supernature, is a pure gift of God. The monk recognizes that fundamental truth and tries to respond to it with the return of his own gift of praise, with a whole life of praise.

Pope Benedict XVI in his social justice encyclical *Caritas in Veritate* wrote: "Because it is a gift received by everyone, charity in truth is a force that builds community, it brings all people together without imposing barriers or limits. …Economic, social and political development, if it is to be authentically human, needs to make room for the *principle of gratuitousness* as an expression of fraternity."[49]

The activity of the monks provides both for the material sustenance of the monastery and makes an economic contribution to the larger human community, but that is not the purpose or motive of the monks' activity, merely a result. Underlying their whole activity is the gratuitous gift of love and life, received and given.

It is worth noting also that in the Middle Ages, the monasteries pretty much served as the "social assistance network" for the poor. Monasteries could be found everywhere, in the city and the countryside. The poor could find at a monastery a handout, a meal, or a bed for the night.

Evidently, the whole of human social order cannot be monastic, but the life of the monastery gives an example

49   *Caritas in Veritate*, 34

that needs to illumine the whole social order. What could
that mean?

There is a famous 19th century painting by the French
painter Jean-François Millet called "The Angelus." The
painting shows two peasants, husband and wife, at the
end of a day of work in the field bowing together in
prayer, with the parish church in the distance. They are
hearing the ringing of the Angelus and saying the prayer.

The monastic life is set up to foster a life of contemplation and praise of God. Ordinary human life of
marriage and of work, while given by God, does not by
itself lead back to God in any obvious way. Nevertheless,
the very simple and beautiful painting shows those two
poles of ordinary human life, marriage and work, brought
back to God, in worship, through prayer. The worship
that takes place in the church reaches out to the activity
in the field, performed together by the married couple,
and together they bring that activity back to the church
by their prayer.

Now, if we consider the village of Fatima in Portugal,
in 1917 shortly before the apparitions of our Lady, the
life of the villagers, represented especially by the families
of the seers, ebbed and flowed from Sunday Mass in the
parish church. They were mostly peasants who worked
in the fields, kept sheep, and tended to their homes and
families. No doubt there was at least a miller, a black-
smith, and shoemaker in the village. Their activity took its
meaning from the Sunday Mass and the hope of heaven.
Even the celebrations from Sunday dinner in the home,
to the celebration of baptisms and weddings, to the village
festival in honor of St. Anthony, revolved around the Mass.
Through family prayer and private prayer they extended
the Mass into their daily life and brought their activity
back as an offering to God in the Mass.[50]

---

50   Sr. Lucia dos Santos wrote about life in the village of Fatima
during her childhood both in her "Memoirs" and in her "Calls
from the Message of Fatima."

Because their actual life fell short, because of their daily sins like gossiping, complaining, lying to one another, and engaging in petty conflicts with each other, the people of Fatima also regularly confessed their sins.

The life of the village was materially poor, filled with much suffering, but also blessed with sufficiency of what was needed, and rich in faith and trust in God. Further the poor but devout families like Sr. Lucia's always had something for those who were poorer than they were.

That basic pattern of Catholic social life that existed in Fatima in 1917, has existed in many times and many places, not just in small villages, but also in cities and towns.

The point is that just as the ordinary human activities of monks in a monastery are taken up and ennobled by being incorporated into a life ordered to the praise of God, the same is possible in a different measure, when the social life of a community revolves around the Sunday Mass in the parish church.

In a similar vein we could consider the building of the great cathedrals of Europe, like Notre Dame of Paris and Notre Dame de Chartres. These were not the products of forced labor. These beautiful edifices rose up from the faith of the people to the glory of God. All the work—not just their work on the cathedral itself - of the architects, stone masons, sculptors, painters, and other craftsmen and laborers, was ennobled by their contribution to the building of the cathedral.

Ordering human life around the Sunday Mass does require a basic simplicity of life, a true spirit of poverty.

Unfortunately, as John Horvat II in his book *Return to Order* rightly observes, modern life is characterized by "frenetic intemperance," a mad desire for "more," for "the latest," for "innovation," for "excitement," that knows no bounds.

If we consider actual science (as opposed to interpretation, questionable theory, and conjecture) there is nothing opposed to the Catholic faith. If we consider technology, it is hard to point to any single device and declare, "It is morally evil." If, however, we consider the scientific and technological culture as a whole, we see the radical disorder of frenetic intemperance, which denying all limits denies God himself. As a result, the culture tears people away from God and blinds them to the reality of God. As a consequence, human life also loses its meaning and value and easily becomes something to be discarded or thrown away when it no longer meets the standards of "utility."

Because we live in such a disordered human society we need a real positive will and determination to impose godly limits upon ourselves, to make the commitment to Sunday Mass the first fundamental limit and acknowledgement of God in our life, and to order our life around that fixed reference point, and, insofar as it lies in our power to do so, build our communities around that fixed reference point.

The first community is the family.[51]

The Foundational Order of the Family

Before continuing now specifically to address the order of the family, the first form of human social life, it will be good to refer once again to the original order of Eden, which was constituted by the hierarchy of man below God, the interior order of the human person, the social order of the marriage between Adam and Eve, and the order of human dominion over the rest of creation.

The Mass works to return man to his right order beneath God and allows God's grace entrance to the

---

[51]   The family is first in order of time; first as the basic material "cell" from which all society is built up. It is not, however, first in the order of perfection because ultimately the family needs larger society for its own perfection and well-being. That indeed is one of the reasons why social justice is needed. Aristotle in his organic exposition of human society starts with the family and builds up to the "State" or "Polis" as the "perfect society", perfect in the sense of self-sufficiency, being endowed with the means necessary to achieve its end. (cf. *Politics*, Bk I, Ch. 2)

human soul, purifying and rectifying the interior order
of the soul. That interior order of the soul is necessary
for the right order of human social relations, especially in
marriage and family life. Nevertheless, I will not address
that interior order of virtue directly, since my purpose is
to write specifically about social justice, the right order
of human society.

All human society begins with the relation between
man and woman in marriage. Jesus called our attention to
the original creation as providing the "law" for marriage,
written in the nature of man from the beginning.[52] When
asked about divorce, he replied,

> Have you not read that from the beginning the
> Creator 'made them male and female' and said,
> 'For this reason a man shall leave his father and
> mother and be joined to his wife, and the two
> shall become one flesh?' So they are no lon-
> ger two but one flesh. Therefore, what God has
> joined, man must not separate.[53]

Jesus refers to two distinct passages from "the beginning." The first comes from Genesis 1. The full passage is:
*God created man in his image; in the divine image he created him;
male and female he created them. God blessed them and said: 'Be
fruitful and multiply; fill the earth and subdue it.*[54] This passage
reveals human marriage very objectively as serving God in
the transmission, we could say, of the divine image from
one generation to the next.

The second passage comes from Genesis 2. The passage
follows from the account of the woman's creation by being
formed from the rib, taken from Adam's side, as a solution
to the original 'solitude of Adam'. *It is not good for man to*

---

52   The exposition here, starting with the words of Jesus and
going from there to the "beginning" follows the basic order of St.
John Paul II's "Theology of the Body."
53   Matt. 19:4–6
54   Gen. 1:27–28

be alone. I will make a suitable partner for him. [55] The passage
is completed by the statement of the transparency and
mutual trust of their relationship: *the man and his wife were
both naked, yet they felt no shame.* [56] This account, we could
say, reveals the union of the two in the intimacy of love
that should be found in marriage.

The teachings contained in Genesis 1 and Genesis 2 are
both essential for understanding the right order of marriage.

Classic theology taught that marriage has a primary end,
the procreation and education of children, and a secondary
end, "mutual help." That was how it was expressed in the
1917 Code of Canon Law. The 1983 Code of Canon Law,
however, merely speaks of marriage being ordered to the
good of the spouses and the procreation and education
of children, in that order, but dropping the language of
"primary" and "secondary" end.

The language of the "ends" and "goals" of marriage
might be clarified a bit if we made reference to the classic
distinction of the "goal of the work" and the "goal of the
one doing the work." [57]

Typically, a young man and young woman are drawn
to marriage first of all because they love each other and
want to share their lives. Yes, they want children together,
but that is probably not what is first of all on their minds.
They are motivated to enter the "good work" of marriage
pursuing their own legitimate goal, stated now as "the
good of the spouses." That is the subjective "goal of the
ones doing the work."

Nevertheless, God, in the first place, established the
"good work" of marriage for the sake of the procreation
and education of children. That is the objective "goal of
the work."

The objective must take priority over the subjective, so
the goal of the work, the procreation and education of

---

55   Gen. 2:18
56   Gen. 2:25
57   *Opus operis* and *opus operantis*

children, must be the primary goal of marriage. We could put it this way, when a man and woman marry, they need to recognize and accept that they are not just engaging in their personal enterprise of life and love, but they are also placing themselves at the service of God, to collaborate with him in bringing into the world and raising up new human beings created in his image and meant to receive his grace so as to become heirs of eternal life. In this way, what is first on their minds is rightly subordinated to the goal intended by God.[58]

Yet, it is not as if the mutual love of the spouses is irrelevant to the primary goal. Far from it: God wants children to come into the world not just as the fruit of the spouses' bodies, but as the fruit of their mutual love. Further, he wants the mutual love of husband and wife to provide children with the nurturing home they need to grow and develop as human beings.

The first creation narrative (Genesis 1) reveals human marriage very objectively as serving God in the transmission, we could say, of the divine image from one generation to the next. The second creation narrative (Genesis 2) reveals the intimacy of love that should be found in marriage.

The subjective order of the intimacy of love must be subordinate to the objective order of the transmission of the divine image (and the life of grace), while at the same time the intimacy of love provides the optimum "cradle" for the transmission of the divine image.

Now let me turn my attention to the objective order of the transmission of human life, created in the divine image. We read: *God created man in his image; in the divine image he created him; male and female he created them. God blessed them and said: "Be fruitful and multiply; fill the earth and subdue it."*[59]

To put the matter simply, the first "work" of man in the order of created nature is simply the multiplication of the

---

58   Cf. Tob. 8:5-7
59   Gen. 1:27-28

divine image through marriage, procreation and education. The simple existence of a human being, a human person, in the image of God, is a great good. In the words of the Second Vatican Council: "Man .... is the only creature on earth which God willed for itself."[60] This good is brought to perfection through the growth and maturation of the human person, but achieves its fullness only through the order of grace by which the human person comes to share, here below, the life of God and, in eternity, the vision and embrace of the Holy Trinity.

Nevertheless, this fundamental work of man of transmitting the divine image is achieved through a twofold participation in that image. *Male and female he created them.*

The male begets a child in a woman, the woman obviously making her own contribution to the material and genetic makeup of the offspring. Pregnancy and motherhood weakens a woman for the sake of the child. In some measure this would be true even if sin had not entered the picture, but in a fallen world the capacity for motherhood is at once both the glory and burden of womanhood. The woman's natural closeness to the child turns her inwards to the home and requires the support of her husband, who is left with the principle responsibility of *subduing the earth* in the service of human need.

Now both the man and the woman are created in God's image. Both are to fulfill their role with intelligence as befits the dignity of that image. To say that a mother's primary role is within the home does not mean that she has no role outside of the home; to say that the man's primary role is outside the home in relation to the world, does not mean that he has no role within the home. Indeed, both father and mother are needed for the proper upbringing of a child.

Nevertheless, the mother's instruction is more oriented to giving the child the fundamental security of belonging, while the father's instruction is more oriented to calling the child out to meet the challenges of the world. This helps us perceive and understand the natural "headship" of the husband, because it is his responsibility to represent and order the family with respect to the larger world. Together they share the care of the common good of the household, but the husband chiefly cares for the integration of the household into a larger whole.

The 3rd and 4th chapters of Genesis show us how the order of marriage and family was disrupted by sin. Through history, deformed by sin, the husband's headship has often degenerated into an abusive lording it over the wife as a mere servant. We must observe also that throughout history, subject to sin, women have often sought to manipulate their husbands for the fulfillment of their own agendas, such as achieving higher social status.

The grace of Jesus Christ brings healing to sin, its inclinations and its effects. This is the context of the two famous passages of St. Paul's Letters to the Ephesians and the Colossians that speak of the wife's subordination to her husband.[61] The larger context of Ephesians begins on this note: *Be imitators of God, as beloved children, and live in love, as Christ love us and handed himself over for us as a sacrificial offering to God for a fragrant aroma.*[62] And Colossians: *If then you were raised with Christ, seek what is above, where Christ is seated at the right hand of God.*[63] When a Christian man and woman, living in grace, both strive to live in the manner set forth by St. Paul in these two letters, the order of man and woman in marriage becomes once again an "order of love," a union of head and heart.[64]

All this being said, it will be necessary to write something about the objective disorders that grace must overcome in order to establish in the family the order of love desired by God

61   Eph. 5:21–33; Col 3:18–21
62   Eph. 5:1–2
63   Col 3:1
64   Cf. *Castii Connubii*, 26–29

THE ORDER OF THE FAMILY SUBJECT TO
"INDUSTRIAL STRENGTH" SOLVENTS

The distinct role of the man and woman precisely in relation to the offspring is what reveals, as a general law of nature, the leadership of the husband in relation to the outside world of "subduing the earth," and the inward looking, domestic role of the wife in making the house to be a true home. This natural order of things, which should be an order of love, was deeply wounded by sin, but like the whole of marriage is healed and restored through the grace of Jesus Christ.

Nevertheless, grace must work in the midst of a fallen world and the modern world has thrown up some particular obstacles to the working of grace. In particular, two radical transformations of modern social life have made the order of love harder, but not impossible, to achieve.

We might think that in the "traditional" order of the family, the husband would go off to work during the day, while the wife stayed home and took care of the house. We are, however, mistaken. Before the industrial revolution the husband was not so separated from the home, nor was the wife so separated from her husband's work. In the life of the country farm and in the life of the urban shop, the husband was never far removed from the home; indeed, the wife collaborated in the work of the husband and the husband's proximity to the home made it easier for him to be a presence in the family.

The industrial revolution changed this by sending the husband off to work in the factory or in the office. He might then come home from a dull, mind-numbing day of work, often weary and exhausted, with little patience for misbehaving children, and little desire for anything but for his wife to serve him dinner.

The wife, on the other hand, was left alone at home. Nevertheless, before the Second World War, the urban wife and mother typically lived in a small, close-knit neighborhood, in which she had the companionship and support of the other housewives. After the Second World War, suburbanization moved the housewife out of the close-knit neighborhood, into the isolation of a somewhat anonymous suburban community, where she was left alone with a new thing—daytime television.

The second radical transformation was presaged during the Second World War, when women supported the war effort by working in factories. Still, it was only in the 1970s that women began entering the workforce in large numbers. Once, jobs were structured with the expectation that a husband and father needed to support wife and family with his salary. Now, that expectation is gone and the economy is structured such that a single paycheck is rarely sufficient.

This movement of women into the workforce was not the result of economic need, but of feminist ideology that set men and women in competition. The working woman, bringing home her own paycheck, was now expected to be more independent of her husband. This brought about the "exaggerated liberty," against which Pope Pius XI warned. An "exaggerated liberty which cares not for the good of the family; it forbids that in this body which is the family, the heart be separated from the head to the great detriment of the whole body and the proximate danger of ruin. For if the man is the head, the woman is the heart, and as he occupies the chief place in ruling, so she may and ought to claim for herself the chief place in love."[65]

In our nation today a boy is not raised to assume the responsibility of providing for a family and taking on the role of a loving and provident husband and father. Nor is a woman prepared to take care of a home and raise children as loving wife and mother. Now society gives no honor or recognition to the dignity of the housewife. Indeed, while 'slut-shaming' is strictly forbidden, the shaming of the stay at home mom is very much in vogue.

---

65 *Casti Connubii*, 27

With both father and mother away from the home and working, children are sent away first to day-care, then to school, where both boys and girls are taught that being adult means "pursuing the career of your choice." When they become young men and women, they begin uniting, often temporarily, often without marriage, on the basis of shared interests. Their union seems to be a sort of sexual companionship while each pursues his or her life goals. That is the new definition of "love" which is readily extended to members of the same sex and which also lends itself to the fantasy world of transgenderism.

Sex becomes the universal escape from the dull machinery of the industrial/technological world that reduces human beings to being cogs in the machine. Children, when they are not an accident of nature—gee, I didn't know that could happen—become a mere afterthought.

"Love" in this view of things does not seem to be very fulfilling. That leads us, then, to the second narrative of creation, which speaks to us of the true intimacy of love: *This one, at last, is bone of my bones and flesh of my flesh.*[66]

The Order of the Intimacy of Love in Marriage

Following the lead of Jesus in his words about divorce, I have gone back to the first chapters of the book of Genesis, to the 'beginning,' to God's original plan for marriage. I noted that Genesis gives us two perspectives on the order of marriage: the objective order of marriage in relation to procreation, which is not a mere physical act, but involves collaborating with God in the transmission of human life, created in his image; and the order of the intimacy of love between husband and wife.

Unfortunately, the untamed might of the industrial revolution has brought us to the pass in which the whole of the western world today seems to move with the inexorable progress of a machine, without any regard for human life.

---

66   Gen. 2:22

We might say that the intimacy of true love, nourished
by divine grace, is the only force in the world capable
of opposing the power of the machine and nourishing
human life. Only now, the love revealed in Genesis, must
be lived in the midst of a fallen, sinful world, and needs
to be purified by the Cross of Christ.

Turning now to the 2nd chapter of Genesis we can
focus on four fundamental points: *It is not good for man
to be alone;*[67] *this at last is bone of my bone and flesh of my flesh;*
[68] *the two shall become one flesh;*[69] *they were both naked and yet
they felt no shame.*[70]

First, the solitude of Adam in the beginning was not an
empty loneliness. Adam was blessed with a life in paradise
and the intimate friendship of God. His solitude possessed
a fulness beyond our experience and comprehension. What
he lacked was someone with whom to share that fulness.
He lacked someone with whom he could share the blessings of God, someone whom he could love as an equal.

So God makes the woman, who will be called Eve, the
mother of the living, as a helper like himself.[71] God
having fashioned the woman from the side of the man,
leads the woman to the man and the man recognizes the
woman as *bone of my bone, flesh of my flesh.* Remarkably what
Adam notes in the woman's body is not the difference in
sex, but the sameness in nature, sharing the same strength
(bone) and the same weakness (flesh).

Yet, obviously the difference in sex is there, the complementarity of the sexes. It is expressed subtly by the
woman being brought to the man, being given to the
man, by God. The woman thus first appears as a gift to
the man, given by God, a gift of God's love, to be loved
by the man.

---

67   Gen. 2:18
68   Gen. 2:22
69   Gen. 2:24
70   Gen. 2:25
71   Gen. 2:18

Here we see beauty and we see danger. On the side of the woman, she is simply brought to Adam, she appears passive. She will need also to give herself. On the side of the man, he could simply take the gift without reciprocating; he must also give himself.

St. John Paul II wrote in this regard:

> The man 'from the beginning' [has] the function of the one who above all receives the gift. The woman has 'from the beginning been entrusted to his eyes, to his consciousness, to his sensibility, to his 'heart'; he by contrast, must in some way ensure the very process of the exchange of the gift, the reciprocal interpenetration of giving and receiving the gift, which, precisely through its reciprocity, creates an authentic communion of persons.[72]

In this first meeting of man and woman, they meet in the body, but what is seen through the body, because of the body, is the person, in the image of God. The "gift" that is exchanged is the gift of the person, in love, expressed through the body. This reciprocity of the gift of the person in love, establishes "an authentic communion of persons." This communion of persons in love, is completed and expressed in the sexual act, the marital act, when the two, who are made for each other, who fit together, become one flesh.

In the beginning, before sin, the body is a transparent expression of the person, the innocent sinless person, the person without ulterior motives, the person ready to give himself or herself in love. That is why two are able to be in each other's presence naked and without shame. Their relationship is transparent; their love is total; they have nothing to hide.

Sin, of course, introduced a disorder within the very person; we are no longer at peace with our own bodies.

---

72   John Paul II, *Theology of the Body*, 17:6

We find ourselves beset by shameful impulses that we want to hide from others. Our will is not upright. We do not act from pure love—especially in the relations between man and woman—but there are a multitude of ulterior motivations.

Still the path of marital love is subject to the same "law of the gift." Only now, the communion of persons expressed in and through the body, in the complementarity of male and female, is something that must be continually built up as the two learn to grow in mutual trust in order to attain evermore the mutual transparency that our first parents had in the beginning.

2

Social Injustice:
The Attack on the Family

SOCIAL JUSTICE AND SEXUAL SINS

On the basis of the first chapters of Genesis, following the lead given by our Lord in his words on divorce, I have written about marriage from the perspective of the objective order of the transmission of human life, created in the image of God, and the subjective order of the intimacy of love in marriage.

This is in the context of social justice, the right order of human society, because marriage and family constitute the first and most fundamental human society. There can be no social justice without the right order of the family. Consequently, the sins that cause disorder in marriage and family should be recognized as sins against social justice. That also means that the separation of the idea of social justice from the right order of family life is itself a grave evil and a violation of true social justice.

So in the light of the order of the transmission of human life and the order of the intimacy of love, it will be good to comment on the sins against marriage and family, in particular the misuse and abuse of human sexual powers and the new life to which they are ordered. All the sins that will be mentioned here are mortal sins that need to be confessed by kind and number to the best of a person's ability.

As a preliminary, though, we need to understand that sexual intercourse properly refers only to the natural sexual union between a man and a woman, because only these two "fit together," and only they can truly unite in a natural sexual act. This is properly called the "marital act" because the only place it can rightly be completed is within the context of the marital commitment.

Any use of sex that is not ordered to completion in a natural sexual union is disordered, incapable of uniting persons, and is not truly an expression of love. The only sort of "love" that can be involved is that of giving each other pleasure, or better helping each other experience pleasure, but there is no communion of persons achieved.

The solitary enjoyment of sexual pleasure has been quite appropriately called "self-abuse." It contains the particular perversity of turning in on oneself a pleasure that is supposed to be the fruit of the love expressed in the marital act. In this light, when two or more people, of the opposite sex or the same sex, consent to enjoy sexual pleasure together apart from true sexual union, it could rightly be called "mutual abuse."

All this procuring of sexual pleasure apart from natural sexual union, besides being essentially sterile and opposed to the order of the transmission of human life, is also unnatural. They are sins against nature created by God.

Next, any natural sexual union that is enjoyed outside of a legitimate marriage lacks the mutual commitment required to establish a true communion of persons in love, fails to express the totality of the gift of self in love, and is performed in complete disregard for the good of any offspring that might result. The couple is not truly "making love," but pretending to "make love," because in one way or another they are holding back and not properly providing for each other and the potential offspring.

All these sins have become common and accepted in today's society. Our youth are left completely without guidance, abandoned to the morality that anything goes, so long as there is consent, just avoid pregnancy and disease.

These sins have become common and accepted, but they still wreak havoc with people's lives. Men and women fail to experience or discover the love they are seeking. They are even deprived of anything close to a right understanding of life. They experience disillusion and frustration and do not know why. Men fail to discover the meaning of their manhood and women fail to discover the meaning of their womanhood. On top of everything, they discover after the fact that they are filled with shame, a confusion of desires, and a polluted imagination. Women are left as single mothers and men are left paying child support for children in whose lives they have little influence. There is often an inheritance of disease or mental illness. In the end people frequently end up hardened, cynical, and embittered, having despaired of ever finding true love. They have at least lost their chance to experience true and pure virginal love.

We need to discover that the "no's" to sexual sins are meant to protect the great "yes" to true and authentic, self-giving love. We need to discover that the prohibitions in regard to sex are not some caprice of God who does not want human beings to experience pleasure (secret: God created pleasure, not the devil). Rather, they are like the levees that channel the force of a mighty river. With the levees in place that mighty force is in the service of life; if the levees are destroyed, that mighty force becomes mightily destructive. In our pride and ignorance, we have gone about destroying the levees. We are now witnessing the destruction far and wide, while we scratch our heads and wonder why.

This is social destruction. Destruction of the right order of human society. This is a matter of social justice.

So far, I have mentioned only sexual sins outside of marriage. I concluded with what is properly called "fornication."

When neither the man or the woman is married the sin is called "fornication," which even though it involves a natural sexual union between a man and a woman, rather than truly "making love" is pretending at "making love." This is because it lacks the commitment of total self-giving and makes no adequate provision for the potential offspring. If fornication is pretending to make love, then cohabitation is "playing house."

The gravity of the evil becomes much more serious when either the man or the woman, or both, are actually married. This is the sin of adultery and contains a specific and grave injustice against the spouse. Every man or woman who has ever entered a marriage with anything approaching a right intention knows that adultery is a radical betrayal of the love and trust that was given to the spouse on the wedding day. It is also a betrayal of the children who have been born of the marriage, who are deprived of the mutual love of their parents. If a child is born of the adultery, that child is from his very conception deprived of the possibility of having his parents married, while the father will be obliged to support that child, depriving his legitimate children of some of the support that is their due. If the mother is married, she might end up imposing on her husband the need to bring up and provide for a child who is not his own.

The will of God is that children be brought into the world through the committed married love of their parents, who will then, in the normal course of things, care for their upbringing. To engage in any action that risks bringing children into the world in any other circumstance is thus a grave injustice and violation of God's law. The present public immorality promotes a culture of adultery and divorce, depriving children of the love of their parents.

We also need to turn our attention to marriage itself, because marriage is not simply a license for sexual pleasure, but a commitment to a mutual self-gift in love, to achieve a communion of persons, in which the man and woman place themselves at God's disposal, to collaborate with his creative power in bringing into the world new human beings created in his image.

Consequently, every use of sex in marriage, every marital act, must serve the communion of persons in love, while remaining open to the gift of life. There is no place for

what I referred to above as "mutual abuse," nor any sort
of contraceptive sex that deliberately frustrates the possibility of a conception.

Contraceptive sex not only violates the laws of the
transmission of life, but also violates the totality of the gift
of self; the husband and wife hold back from each other
their generative capacity, their ability to become a father
or mother. In the end, contraceptive sex likens the natural
sexual union to the various forms of "mutual abuse." Without openness to life, true sexual union is not really achieved.

In contrast to contraception, which places a positive
obstacle in the way of the generation of life, thereby trun-
cating the marital act, both physically and in its meaning
and purpose, natural family planning, which is based on
making use of the woman's natural cycle of fertility, does
nothing to the act itself, except observe the time, an
external circumstance. If, in order to space births, for a
legitimate reason, the couple has recourse to the woman's
infertile periods, they are completely giving themselves
to each other, such as they are at the time.

How about couples who are sterile, whether by physical
defect or by age? If marriage is ordered to the transmission of life, why are they allowed to marry? Here I think it
is necessary to admit that a couple that knowingly enters
into a sterile marriage do not sin, enter into a true marriage, but fall short of the full meaning of marriage. Still,
they are capable of achieving the communion of persons
in love through the marital act and are engaging in the
same sort of act that, in other circumstances is capable
of bringing forth life, while not putting any obstacle to
the generation of life.

The Josephite marriage (which in one unique miracu-
lous instance, from which this type of marriage draws its
name, bore a child) is another matter altogether, since by
mutual consent the couple refrains from the marital act
altogether for a higher good, mutual help in belonging
completely to God.

We would do well to call upon St. Joseph, the head of the Holy Family, to intercede for us and lead us away from and protect us from the ruinous destruction of our culture and lead us towards a saner, healthier, holier family life in accord with God's plan.

SOCIAL JUSTICE AND SINS AGAINST THE BEGINNING OF HUMAN LIFE

Disordered uses of sex, as sins against marriage, are violations of social justice. Next, it is necessary to address the grave injustices that bear on the human life itself that is generated. Already, with contraception, man begins an attempt to wrest the springs of life from the hands of God, but with the crimes that follow man truly begins to take the place of God.

The first, best known, and most obvious, is what very often takes place when contraception fails—and it does fail—namely abortion, the grave crime that is nothing less than a murder of an innocent human being at its most vulnerable and in the one place where, by rights, it should be the most protected.

Since Roe v. Wade there have been 61 million abortions in the United States.[1] While the number of abortions has dropped significantly in recent years, the annual average has been about 1.3 million. As late as 1997 it actually exceeded heart disease and cancer combined as the leading cause of death. Now it has fallen to 2nd place behind heart disease. Still that is more than 600,000 abortions too many each year.

I write very objectively about the nature of the crime. The woman who seeks an abortion, however, very often, far from choosing freely, feels she has no options. That is the testimony of Abby Johnson, former Planned Parenthood clinic director, who herself had two abortions.

The woman who seeks an abortion has, in the first place, been abandoned by a society that first has declared

---

1   Since writing this *Roe v. Wade has been overturned. Abortion is now illegal in many States, but in others there are no legal limits on abortion.*

a "right" to abortion and now even begins to celebrate abortion. The society in which she lives, far from deterring her from having an abortion, leaves her, in the moment of a grave crisis in her life, with the door open and even encourages her to walk through that door, while leaving her in the dark as to what she is doing and what the consequences will be. Further, the woman is very often abandoned by the father of the child and even pressured at times by her own parents. Very often there is hardly a person so alone and abandoned in the world as a woman who chooses to have an abortion. Then she must live the rest of her life with the knowledge of what she has done to her own child—a knowledge that even God's forgiveness in the confessional cannot extinguish—and how by extinguishing the life in her womb she profoundly violated her own nature and dignity as a woman.

Those most guilty here are the politicians, judges, lawyers, and celebrities, especially the ones who call themselves Catholic, who have established and maintain the abortion regime. It is a great disgrace that so many Catholics who pride themselves on their social justice credentials fail to recognize the gravity of abortion as a social justice issue. The supposed right to an abortion undercuts the very possibility of a right social order and has radically corrupted the fields of medicine, law, and politics. This is truly a crime that calls to God for vengeance.[2]

Abortion extinguishes the life conceived in the womb, but "in-vitro" fertilization takes the generation of life away from the marital act and turns a human being into a laboratory product rather than the offspring of the loving union of husband and wife. Indeed, so far is this from the loving union of husband and wife that the man's contribution must be obtained by "self-abuse."

There is no right to have a child. A child does not belong first to his parents, but to God, the Creator. The parents are not the masters of procreation, but in the procreative

---

2   Cf. CCC 1867, cf. Rev. 6:10

act, they place themselves at the service of God. If God chooses not to create a new life through them, even after much prayer and supplication, and even after recourse to every legitimate medical means, there is nothing left for them to do but humbly submit to the will of God.

"In-vitro" fertilization is bad enough when it is employed by a legitimate husband and wife, but the levels of perversity mount when someone else's womb is "rented" as a surrogate mother and when, even worse, it is put at the service of providing same sex couples with children, turning the same sex relationship even more into an obscene mockery of holy matrimony.

In addition, there are the embryos (that is, tiny human beings) that are inevitably destroyed as part of the process and the other innumerable embryos that are frozen indefinitely. Many of those frozen embryos are no longer wanted and many no longer even have legitimate parents, meaning there is no longer any legitimate way to bring them to term. The holy angels weep. The Holy Virgin Mary, Mother of God weeps. Jesus weeps.

Social Justice and Gender Ideology

After writing about the right order of marriage and the family, based on Jesus' words that direct us to the story of creation in Genesis, I began the grim but needed task of cataloguing the sins against the right order of the family. These sins, involving disorders of sexual practice and attacks against human life at its most vulnerable stage, in the womb, are sins against social justice.

Since all manner of sexual promiscuity, cohabitation, contraception, abortion, and IVF have become so much part and parcel of the society we live in, often backed up by legislation and court rulings, we live in a society that, at its very core, has given way to a radical social injustice. We live in a society that far from upholding and promoting the right order of marriage and family life seeks rather to overturn and obliterate that order at every turn. The family that seeks to live in accord with God's plan is now the target of attack (often legal) and shaming.

Alas, we are not yet done. With the societal promotion and protection of the family broken down, with the very meaning of male and female thrown into confusion, we are now being inundated with "gender ideology," which subordinates "sex assigned at birth" to a person's self-determined "gender identity" and would require everyone else to recognize and honor that "gender identity."

Gender ideology actually has its roots in radical feminist ideology, even though some radical feminists, because they still define a woman by her body, are opposed to the transgender movement.

The radical feminism of the 60s and 70s, which has been very pervasive in its societal influence, was built on the premise that biological differences between male and female were insignificant, and that cultural paradigms of masculinity and femininity were purely "social constructs." To put the matter simply, if little boys liked playing with toy soldiers and little girls like dressing up dolls, that is only because of societal expectations. The claim is that masculinity and femininity is all a matter of nurture and not at all a question of nature. The further claim is that "nurture" has been for the sake of keeping women in subjugation to patriarchal domination. The whole purpose of their argument was to free women from their biology (their physical weakness in comparison to men and their ability to get pregnant) so as to compete with men on equal terms in all realms of politics and economics.[3]

This radical feminism has always been profoundly hostile to marriage and family (though it has not always been upfront about its hostility). If marriage and family has had any acceptance it has only been on the supposition

---

3   Have there been real abuses and injustices that occasioned the rise of radical feminism? Most certainly. Nevertheless, feminism has exploited those abuses not to restore order, but to destroy the great good of marriage and family life.

of an equality of roles (men and women equally share cooking and cleaning) and equality of decision making. Children can only be allowed into the "arrangement" if and when the woman so desires, otherwise she is to be absolute mistress of her fertility.

Still, radical feminism, even if it sought a radical equality between men and women, did not finally try to deny the male-female duality. The transgender movement, however, goes much further by rejecting "heteronormativity" and "gender binarism."

We can get an idea of how radical the transgender movement is by comparison to radical feminism if we consider Title IX of the federal Education Amendments Act of 1972, a classic piece of feminist legislation.

The key principle was, "No person in the United States shall, on the basis of sex, be excluded from participation in, be denied the benefits of, or be subjected to discrimination under any education program or activity receiving Federal financial assistance."

Among other things, this required equal funding for women's sports programs in comparison with men's sports programs, because it rejected any possibility that sports might be more important for the growth and development of boys into young men than it is in the development of girls into young women.

At the same time Title IX tacitly acknowledged a certain inequality, because women's sports programs would remain separate from men's programs. Here women were not expected to compete against men. They were just granted an equal right to compete among each other.

Title IX also recognized the need for different facilities (locker rooms and bathrooms) for men and women.

The Obama Administration embraced the transgender movement, opened up the military to transgenderism, and sought to reinterpret Title IX, unsuccessfully for the time being, replacing "sex" with "gender." This would have given men a "right" to compete in women's sports, so long as they claim to be women (which is already taking place anyway) and a "right" to use women's bathrooms, so long as they claim to be women (which is already taking place anyway). This reinterpretation throws out all the ways that Title IX still recognized the importance of some biological inequality and sought to protect women in their vulnerability. It thereby completely repurposes the whole legislation, turning it into a tool to eliminate sexual distinction from human life.

If radical feminism sought a radical equality between men and women, it did not finally try to deny the male-female duality.

The transgender movement, however, has adopted the basic principle of feminism, namely that gender is nothing more than a social construct, with no real roots in "nature," or at least no relevant roots in nature, and taken it further. If gender is no more than a social construct, then there is no reason why a man might not decide he is really a woman or a woman decide that she is really a man. The body is irrelevant. If the person with a man's body wants to adopt the social construct of "femininity" for his identity, that is his right. Further, if he wants even to modify his body accordingly, why not? Further, if gender is only a social construct, why only two genders? Why not a whole "gender spectrum."

Now, while I have followed the basic logic of the argument, we should not look too closely at the logic, because the logic is purely in service of the ideology. So, on the one hand, the transgender movement will argue that people were born a certain way (male person in a female body) and since they have no power over the matter, should be accommodated. Then they will turn around and declare that a person has a right to choose their gender, that no gender should be forced on anyone, much less should any gender be "assigned" at birth.

But let's return to the basic premise, that gender is no more than a social construct, pure nurture and no nature.

Not only is the premise patently wrong (just consider that little girls like to look at faces, but little boys like to look at things), but also it is extremely destructive of children.

The destructive character of gender ideology is brought to absurd and tragic extremes when toddlers are allowed to choose their "gender," prepubescent children are given "puberty blockers" (powerful drugs whose long term effects are little understood, but generally will cause sterility) to "block" the unwanted development of their bodily sex, and teenagers are given cross-sex hormones (also powerful drugs) and even allowed to choose self-mutilating surgery to conform their body to the likeness of their chosen gender. This is extreme child abuse in more ways than one. This is not only a failure of the guidance due to children, it is positive misguidance.

Guidance and, we could say, true education are necessary for the nurture of human nature. Boys are meant to grow to be men and girls are meant to grow to be women, but while the biological growth follows from a basic minimum of nutrition and health care, the full human growth and maturation is a most delicate process and one that is far from certain in its outcome.

The basic maturity for a man is that he is capable of entering into a marriage and becoming a reasonably decent husband and father; the basic maturity for a woman is that she is capable of entering into marriage and becoming a reasonably decent wife and mother. That means that a young man and a young woman, by their 20th year at most, are capable of making the lifetime commitment of marriage.

Nevertheless, because of radical feminism, we already threw out sex-specific education. If boys have been guided to become men, it is only because of what they received in their family; if girls have been guided to become women, it is only because of what they received in their family. Nevertheless, those family structures have been under incessant attack, while the schools, giving expression to public policy, only prepare boys and girls indifferently to pursue a "career," a life of work.

Between the schools (sex-education) and the popular culture teenagers learn that, in regard to sex, anything goes between consenting adults, only they should avoid pregnancy and avoid disease. That is our current public sexual morality.

This has left children with no basic capacity to tell the difference between right and wrong in one of the most basic areas of human life, the most basic realm of human social life. This has left children clueless as to what marriage is all about, though nature inevitably inclines them towards marriage.

This fundamental confusion has come from abandoning one of the most fundamental tasks of education; leaving children without guidance, left to figure things out for themselves, has led us to this ultimate degree of confusion about basic human reality that is revealed in the celebration of the transgender movement.

Social Justice Corrupted by Equality Without Truth

I have written about the Mass and the family as the two basic principles of true social justice. Then, I began writing about the different sins that attack the family in various ways, and thereby undermine social justice. This led to a discussion of the transgender movement, which is rooted in the same principle as radical feminism, namely that gender is a pure social construct, independent of biological sex. Here we begin to see that the right order of the family, as a true principle of social justice has been attacked in the name of social justice. Here we begin to see that what the world today calls "social justice" actually masks the most radical social injustice.

All this has come about in the name of "equality", a key term in the world's language of "social justice." When the world speaks of social justice it begins with "equality." If there is inequality, there is injustice that must be eradicated.

There is a partial truth here because indeed equality is bound up with the understanding of justice, but not an undifferentiated equality. The classic standard of justice is "to each his own." The equality is between a person and what is "owed" to him in some sense. There are ways in which all human persons are equal, but there are also many ways in which they are unequal (and rightly so). The first and most obvious inequality is between parents and their children. There is nothing unjust about that inequality.

Indeed, an ordered society (and so a rightly ordered society) is impossible without inequality, because where there is order (apart from the 1st, 2nd, and 3rd persons of the Holy Trinity) there is some sort of inequality. Right order brings unequal elements into a harmonious unity. That means that before we can understand just equality, we must understand the nature of things and their just order. Before equality, justice is based on truth and truth is rooted in reality.

Contemporary ideologies, by blurring distinctions and denying or obscuring the truth, upset all right order attacking not only unjust inequalities, but also legitimate inequalities and privileges.

The transgender movement, with its blatant denial of the fundamental reality of sexual differentiation and its importance in human life, is the latest, most absurd, and most tragic fruit of the wrongheaded worship of "equality."

It also attacks one of the most fundamental truths of creation, *male and female he made them*, and therefore radically denies the truth and reality of the Creator.[4]

The truth of male and female should be evident to the human reason, but in a time when this fundamental truth of human life has been thrown into confusion, divine revelation becomes more important.

The first chapter of Genesis reveals to us the great order of the created world, with man, created in God's image, male and female, at the summit of the visible creation. All

4   Gen. 1:27

things are ordered to man, man rules over the physical world as God's "steward," but man himself is ordered to the worship of God (the seventh day), so he also serves as the "priest" of the physical world.

None of this is in any way contrary to science, as I have already argued. Rather it reveals to us the meaning and purpose of the created world, something beyond the scope of a science that can reach only the surface "facts" of the sequence, structure, and mechanics of the visible world.

The second chapter of Genesis, as already noted, reveals the order of the four fundamental harmonies that were disrupted by sin. Man below God, the interior order of the human person, the relation between man and woman, and the relation between man and the lower creation.

True justice can never be achieved by seeking an artificial, undifferentiated equality, as though there were no intrinsic order either in the created world or in human society; rather true justice seeks the right order in each of the four mentioned realms, beginning with the subordination of man to God in right worship, the Holy Sacrifice of the Mass.

SOCIAL JUSTICE AND DIVORCE

I have written about social justice, the right order of human social life, built around two pillars, public worship of God in the Holy Sacrifice of the Mass and marriage and family life as the first society. I have also written about the various cultural attacks against the integrity of marriage: sexual sins, sins against procreation and life, and the transgender attack on the fundamental distinction of the sexes. Nevertheless, I have yet to expand upon the fundamental sin against marriage itself: Divorce.

Divorce goes directly against the explicit teaching of Jesus Christ, rooted in the original creation of man, male and female. In answer to the Pharisees' question about divorce, which was tolerated by the law of Moses, Jesus replied:

> Have you not read that he who made man from the beginning, made them male and female? And he said, 'For this reason shall a man leave father and mother and cleave to his wife, and the two shall become one flesh. Therefore they are not two, but one flesh. What therefore God joined together, let no man put asunder.[5]

Then when asked about the permission Moses gave, Jesus replied:

> Because Moses by reason of the hardness of your heart permitted you to put away your wives, but from the beginning it was not so. And I say to you that whoever shall put away his wife, except it be for fornication, and shall marry another, commits adultery, and he that shall marry her that is put away, commits adultery.[6]

NEITHER NULLITY NOR SIMPLE SEPARATION ARE DIVORCE

Before entering more deeply in this matter it will be good to mention two things that are not divorce: nullity and simple separation.

The first involves a question that develops directly from the words of Jesus, which seem to allow for an exception.

Much has been made of this "exception," which is here translated literally as "fornication." There are two ways of understanding this "exception," both of which mean the same thing in the end.

One is that fornication, sex between a man and woman who are not married, by definition, is impossible for someone who is truly married. The sin for a married person would be adultery, not fornication. Hence to speak of fornication (meaning the supposed "husband" and "wife" were actually engaged in fornication) as grounds for a divorce, effectively means that the marriage was not a true marriage.

---

5 Matt. 19:4–6
6 Matt. 19:8–9

The other interpretation traces the Greek word *porneia* back to a conjectured Hebrew or Aramaic original and sees it as referring to marriages that were forbidden in Mosaic law on account of their being incestuous. Once again, it means the marriage was not a true marriage to begin with. The "New American Bible" authorized by the United States Conference of Catholic Bishops translates the exception as "unless the marriage is unlawful". That faithfully renders the true meaning of the exception.

In any case, the proper interpretation, guaranteed by Catholic tradition, means that in the case of a true marriage Jesus' prohibition of divorce is absolute.

Nevertheless, there might be some things that have the outward appearance of a marriage but are not. That would eventually become the foundation for the Church's process for declaring some marriages "null" or "invalid." The declaration of nullity, wrongly referred to as "annulment," is a judgment regarding the moment of entering the marriage that something was lacking for the establishment of a true marriage, hence a true marriage did not result, hence the two are not bound by the commitment of marriage.

Divorce, however, pretends to take what is supposed to be a true marriage and declares that it no longer exists. Divorce by intention destroys an existing marriage. That is the fundamental malice of divorce.

That said much criticism has been leveled against the Church's "annulment process," especially in the United States, where it is widely perceived as a form of Catholic divorce. Here it is important to grasp that the principle underlying the process itself—namely that there can be relationships that had the public appearance of being true marriages, but were lacking some essential element, thus rendering them "invalid"—is sound. The Church's legal process, however, is subject both to the human fallibility of the judges as well as the possibility of corruption, which can enter at any level, from the giving of evidence, to the reporting of evidence, to the recording of evidence, to the actual judgment itself.

Practically speaking, anyone who enters the process in good faith can act on the result in good conscience. The same cannot be said for someone who gets the result they want by exploiting, manipulating, or corrupting the process. A human tribunal can be deceived, but God is never deceived.

It is also necessary to distinguish between divorce and simple separation. To put the matter simply: a husband and wife are obliged to live together, but while divorce should not be regarded as an option, a separation of the common life, even a permanent one, might at times be justified. Yet, presuming the validity of the marriage itself, neither is free to enter a new marriage.

This is important because while the Church urges husband and wife to reconcile, or at least keep open the hope of reconciliation, in situations of physical or moral danger, or situations of infidelity, an injured spouse is not obliged to maintain the common life. The Church has never held, for example, that a wife must at all costs submit to grave abuse and injury from her husband.

Properly in these matters recourse should be had to the bishop and not to civil courts, especially when the latter have little understanding of the truth of marriage, but, alas, in the United States, at least, it appears that the bishops have failed to assert their authority and have neglected their responsibility.[7]

The practical result of all this is that when the common life of marriage falls apart, Catholics have recourse to civil divorce at the very least to settle matters pertaining to finances and custody of children. Then, regardless of the intentions entering the divorce, the newly acquired "single" status and the language that refers to the "ex", helps shape a mindset that the marriage indeed no longer exists, that it is time to move on, and maybe find a new partner.

---

7 Cf. Code of Canon Law 1151-1155

THE EVIL OF DIVORCE

We really need to set aside political correctness and the fear of offending so as to be clear about the evil of divorce.

What I shall write on this subject is not meant to be a blanket condemnation of those who have been involved in divorces any more than an exposition of the evil of abortion is meant to be a blanket condemnation of women who have had abortions.

In both cases, individuals are caught up in a cultural storm in which, even if they have failed, even if they have given in to their weakness, even if they have been selfish, they have also been abandoned to their weakness and encouraged in their selfishness by the culture in which they live, many times by their closest friends as well. At the same time, while the Church has upheld the teaching of Christ on a theoretical level, her ministers, acting "pastorally," have themselves often been complicit in the divorce culture.

Nevertheless, unless we learn to speak clearly and objectively of the evils involved, we will never get out of the mess we have fashioned for ourselves.

If we recall that the first purpose of marriage is the procreation and education of children, then we can grasp that the first and most obvious evil is the incalculable harm done to children. It is also a betrayal of the love to which the couple committed themselves on their wedding day. Divorce inevitably contains an element of despair that is not found in a mere "separation" that acknowledges the permanence of the marriage bond.

DIVORCE HARMS CHILDREN

First, let us consider the harm done to the children. This harm is real and objective, even when the children are little aware of it, even when a variety of circumstances seem to compensate in some way or another.

Every child has a father and mother: that remains true even if modern scientific perversions are capable of reducing the father to being merely a "sperm donor" and the mother to being an "egg donor." The father and mother are the human origin of the child whose genetic inheritance is received from them.

There are all sorts of tragic reasons, beyond human control that result in a child losing his father or mother, or both. Already because of this an orphan is deeply wounded. The whole biblical tradition urges us to compassion and mercy for those who are so wounded. There can also be such radical failures on the part of the father or mother that do indeed require outside intervention that will sometimes lead to the child having to be removed from the home. That too leaves a deep wound in the child; even the best adoptive parents or the best foster parents really cannot substitute for what the father and mother should have been. Here, though, we are speaking about the physical and even moral tragedies that have always been part of the human condition.

It is something altogether different when a child is deprived of either father or mother by a definite human choice, especially when it is the choice of either or both of the parents. If a child who loses his father to an accidental death often feels that his father abandoned him, then how can he not, on some level, feel that his divorced parents (or one of them at least) actually reject him.

The whole of healthy human psychology is founded on human origins: the father and mother. Their division leaves the child divided within himself; their hatred leaves the child struggling with self-hatred. All sorts of other circumstances can mask over the wound, but I would dare say it is always there.

Further, all this is exacerbated by social, cultural, and legal structures that encourage divorce and so leave the child abandoned not only by his parents, but also by the whole of the society to which he is born.

Of course, God can heal and transform all wounds, but that doesn't mean we should intentionally inflict wounds so that God can heal them.

Be that as it may, we have become a society that on the one hand idolizes children and on the other hand abandons them. The idolization seems to be a sort of guilty "compensation" for the abandonment. We tell children how great they are, how deserving they are, and we shower them with gifts, but we deprive them of the one thing they most need—and deep down most want—a father and mother who are married to each other and who love each other.

I have heard the heart wrenching scream of a child, "Why did you have to get divorced!" I have heard a child of divorce give an eloquent talk that boiled down to, "You have to look out for yourself in life, because no one else will." That is what divorce teaches children; that is what the whole divorce culture teaches children.

DIVORCE STRIKES AT THE INTIMACY OF LOVE BETWEEN HUSBAND AND WIFE

Divorce also strikes at the intimacy of love promised by husband and wife on their wedding day.

In Paris, France, there used to be a bridge to which couples from all over the world would come in order to fasten a lock to the bridge, as a symbol of their undying love; often the couple would even throw the key into the river Seine. Regardless of the actual reality and solidity of the love professed by these couples, their action bears witness to the universality and depth of desire for a marital union built upon an unbreakable love.

I would say that usually, unless there are ulterior motives (like money, fear, or appearance), when a young man and young woman get married they desire to unite their whole lives in an unbreakable bond of love. Even when they are hedging their bets they do so because they are afraid the actual marital life will not work out, while deep down they long for the unbreakable bond. If they do not give themselves to each other completely, it is not that they lack the desire for such a totality of love, but because they are afraid of being hurt.

Further, there is something truly remarkable, eminently human, and authentically noble in the way that a marriage is established. The man and woman give their word to each other in the presence of witnesses, divine and human. The man and woman give themselves to each other through their pledged word. Properly and humanly a man and woman should give themselves to each other through their word, before they give their bodies to each other. Properly and humanly the bodily union of the marital act should be an expression of the pledged word given at the wedding. The undying love that is sought in marriage is a love that is rooted in a pledged word and in the mutual trust in the pledge that was given.

While simple separation holds on to the hope of reconciliation, which keeps the undying love alive, if only by the thinnest thread, divorce involves the definitive rejection of the pledge. Adultery betrays the pledge in act but does not deny the pledge in principle. Divorce is the ultimate infidelity to the irrevocable pledge that was once given, pretending to render it void altogether.

This is what divorce does, of itself. What we have now is not just the possibility of divorce under very strict conditions, but a divorce culture rooted in the legal concept of "no-fault divorce," which makes it very easy for one party to the marriage to exit unilaterally. It has been said that marriage is now the only contract for which there is no legal obligation; either party to the contract can violate or render the contract void at will.

THE CULTURE OF DIVORCE: A CULTURE OF FALSEHOOD, INFIDELITY, AND ISOLATION

Yet, if we speak of marriage as a contract, it is the most fundamental contract of all. If the marriage contract has been rendered meaningless, what is the binding force behind any other contract? If a man and woman are not bound to their word in marriage, how can they be bound to their word in any other circumstance? If the pledged word of the marriage bond is empty, what becomes of truth telling in general? Words no longer have any meaning except to construct fantasy worlds in which we may live as we please and destroy as we please. Life becomes like a virtual reality game. If it doesn't work out, we can exit and start another game.

This culture of falsehood and unreality produced by the divorce culture attacks and undermines all marriages. Those preparing for marriage, with hopes and desires for an unbreakable bond of love, have their hopes undermined from the beginning because they grew up with the experience of divorce and because their desire, planted in their hearts by God, seems unrealistic. Those trying to live a true and faithful marriage instead of finding the support they need to persevere, to meet the challenges, and overcome the difficulties, find themselves abandoned by the larger society that makes it easy for them and in various ways encourages them to exit and move on.

Since marriage is the first and most fundamental human society, the first society in which a man or woman cease to be a mere individual and become part of a greater unity, the weakening and dissolution of marriage tends to reduce all of society to an assembly of individuals perpetually trying to negotiate relationships to fulfill personal need and convenience, but without any real bond between them—certainly no lasting bond. The divorce culture has opened wide the door to radical individualism and the isolation and loneliness that entails.

3
The Meaning and Purpose of Work

An Introduction to the Dignity of Work

There are three great marvels in the natural order of human life: children who have been well brought up; a woman who is happily married; a man who finds satisfaction in his work, without neglecting his wife and children. These three marvels are obviously interrelated and when they all come together they make for a fourth marvel, a happy family. These marvels belong to the natural order, but they are scarcely achievable without the aid of supernatural grace.

Yes, a woman can find gainful employment outside of the home and a woman can also be a happy mother, nevertheless, apart from a happy nun or woman religious—and that involves the supernatural order and a different kind of marriage—what, for the most part, really seems to bring fulfillment to a woman in this life is marriage. If the marriage fails or is not found, there is no substitute.

Not even motherhood seems to fulfill a woman as does marriage; a woman can be a great mother, struggling either as a single mother or enduring a difficult marriage, but she is deeply hurting because she does not have the love of her husband.

While a woman by no means needs to be limited to the home, a woman can truly find fulfillment and satisfaction within the home in a way that a man usually cannot. For a man, while marriage and fatherhood are also important and central for his natural human fulfillment, the man typically needs something more, a work, a task, a mission.

Typically, when a woman finds herself obliged to work full time in order to support her family, she experiences an intense conflict between the demands of the family and work.

For a man, however, working to support his wife and family is one of the main ways that he shows his love for his family. This very masculine instinct goes awry when the man thinks that he has fulfilled his role as husband and father merely by putting food on the table. Nevertheless, when the man is unable to provide for his family by means of his work, he suffers a deep interior frustration and sense of uselessness. Things are very different if a man finds his work frustrating or unfulfilling but is nevertheless able to provide for his family. Precisely because he is able to provide for his family, he is often able to find meaning in the sacrifice he makes. He endures the hard work, the grind, the humiliation for the love of his family.

This is all reflected—both the right order and the disorder—in the punishment God pronounced on Adam and Eve in Genesis. The woman is to experience suffering in childbearing and in relation to her husband; she suffers from the disorder of sin in what most touches her womanhood.[1] The man experiences suffering in his work: *By the sweat of your face you shall get your bread to eat.*[2]

This leads us into another realm of social justice: work and economic organization. Here we enter into a realm that is more traditionally identified with social justice; indeed, the workingman was at the center of the considerations in the foundational social encyclical of Pope Leo XIII, *Rerum Novarum*.

Nevertheless, the economic issues have become so dominant that they have usually lost the needed context of religion and family. Once again in Eden there were four original harmonies that were disrupted by sin: man beneath God, the interior order of man, man and woman, man and the world. Work (and so also economy) belong to the last harmony.

---

1   Gen. 3:16
2   Gen. 3:19

There is a great deal of complexity here, especially in our contemporary world. My intent in what follows is to offer first a few reflections on man's relation to work, then on his relation to the world/environment through his work.

I do not intend so say much about economic organization, except to highlight the priority of work. The "lockdowns" introduced as a response to the Covid pandemic caused massive unemployment, deprived millions of their jobs, their work. No amount of stimulus payments can compensate the loss of work. The loss of work does not just mean the loss of income, it means the loss of meaningful activity.

A great deal of discussion regarding measures to be taken for the sake of national prosperity revolve around not the worker, but the consumer. One of the great measures of American prosperity is Black Friday retail sales. That is disordered. It reveals that we have an economy ruled by consumerism, not by the dignity of work.

THE NOBILITY OF WORK

Work, rather than consumption, should be central to economic organization; work is not just a matter of income and making a living; work, especially for men, is meaningful activity.

Many people are familiar with the prophecy of Isaiah: *They shall beat their swords into plowshares and their spears into pruning hooks.*[3] It is part of a larger passage, the whole of which needs to be understood. The prophet Micah has the very same prophecy, but with an additional line that bears upon work: *Every man shall sit under his own vine or under his own fig tree, undisturbed.*[4]

The whole prophecy, one of the great revelations of true social justice and the peace that flows from it, follows the same order as my entire exposition of the subject. First

3   Isa. 2:4
4   Mic. 4:4

is the priority of the Lord's house, the right worship of God.[5] God then instructs the peoples in the right way of living.[6] The family is passed over, but in Micah, at least it is included in the final line because behind "every man" sitting under his vine or fig is the wife and family he supports; the whole family is represented by the father of the family. Before we get there, though, the law of God directs men away from conflict and war (the work of warfare) to the cultivation of the land, the work of peace. The result is that each man comes to enjoy the fruit of his labors represented by the vine and the fig. The man's domain is not plundered either by raiders (as often happened in ancient Israel) or by fraud and extortion (another frequent occurrence). Of course, the final reward of "work" comes from God himself *who will repay each man according to his works.*[7]

Let us focus for a moment on the vine and fig: this represents the works of peace. Let us expand the image slightly with another passage from Isaiah: *They shall live in the houses they build, and eat the fruit of the vineyards they plant.*[8]

By these two works, building and planting, a man fulfills his most basic needs, food and shelter. Food, however, is more than just nourishment it is the great symbol of shared life, friendship, and joy. A house is not just protection from the elements, but is the home, the place of security, comfort, rest, not just for the man himself, but for his family.

By his work, then, a man has the satisfaction for providing for his needs, the needs of his family, and men are brought together into the life of a community.

The planting and cultivating the earth is the most primitive and characteristic biblical occupation of man. It is contained both in the ancient command, *Fill the earth*

5   Isa. 2:1–3; Mic. 4:1–2
6   Isa. 2:3–4; Mic. 4:2–3
7   Rom. 2:6, cf. Matt. 16:27
8   Isa. 65:21

and subdue it and in Adam's placement in Eden *to till the garden and keep it.*[9]

I would suggest that one of the great disorders of the modern world is the displacement of the population from the land to massive cities, followed by the conversion of excellent farmland into housing developments and shopping malls. I think it was only in about 1950 that the majority of the population of the United States was living in urban areas. It has only been since 2000, if I am not mistaken, that the majority of the world population tipped in the same direction. That may actually be the most staggering demographic fact of the world in which we live today.

The pandemic has forcefully set before our eyes that agricultural work, though despised, is truly essential. There is also a special fulfillment in agricultural work—despite its uncertainty and frustration—that is revealed in the unique joy of the harvest. A priest who ministered to migrant workers once recounted to me that a cherry picker once proudly told him about how many tons of cherries his team had picked that day and that by the following day those cherries would be on tables throughout the world. The worker then said, "We are feeding people." I also once read of a migrant worker who picked various crops and who liked going into the produce sections of supermarkets. Why? To admire his handiwork!

We see now that the reward for the worker that goes far beyond just putting food on his own table. He perfects himself and contributes to the good of others. There is something inherently ennobling about honest work well done.

The greatest example of this is none less than St. Joseph, who by his labors provided for the Immaculate Mother of God and for the very Son of God made man, our Savior Jesus Christ. Further, Jesus himself not only was willing to be known as *the son of the carpenter* but also took up the labor himself. When God created the world by the

9   Gen. 1:28; 2:15

command of his word there was no sweat or toil involved, but when a man, even the Son of God made man, works in the created world, he collaborates with God the Creator and reflects in a small way his glory.

WORK THAT IS MEANINGFUL, PERSONAL, AND TRULY HUMAN

There is something inherently noble about honest work well done, but the process of industrialization and "technologization" has emptied much work of its meaning.

Assembly lines are famous for their dehumanizing character. In the United States the service industry has replaced manufacturing. Now we have the new assembly lines of Amazon Fulfillment Centers; we have customer service call centers and Costco greeters that require infinite patience and a paste-on smile as people must represent a vast impersonal organization that has little connection with any local community. Very often a person might be left wondering if they are serving other persons, or only the vast machinery of production and distribution. Meanwhile, more and more human activity is replaced by the computer and robot.

Work is more meaningful the closer the workman is to the product or the "servant" to the one served. So, the more machines, rather than just simple tools, insert themselves between the workman or the craftsman and the finished product, the more the workman or craftsman is reduced to being a mere operator of machinery, which does the real work, so to speak.

As for the product, what has been made, the more directly it is the work of human hands, the more it ceases to be merely functional and becomes a bearer of meaning and beauty. The machine is efficient and produces a mass quantity of identical useful items, but they lack the "stamp" of a person. Each handmade item is specifically the product of a person who made that very item.

Sr. Lucia of Fatima made rosaries for the missions; each rosary was a work not only of her hands, but also of her own prayers. In that way, through the rosary, her prayers and her love, reached those who would come to use those rosaries, even though she never met them.

Contrariwise, Milton Friedman spoke of the marvels of free-market capitalism in a single pencil, pointing out that the pencil was ultimately the product of workers throughout the world. What he missed, however, is that each of those workers was so removed from the final product that his intention could scarcely reach the anonymous pencil user at the other end. Indeed, many of those workers were probably completely unaware that some part of their work would end up in pencils being sold in a distant part of the world.

The person who prayed with a rosary made by Sr. Lucia, prayed with a rosary that had been made personally and intended for use by a person living in "mission territory." The user of a pencil makes use of an impersonal product to which countless persons happened to contribute.

The old-fashioned village shoemaker, made shoes for those he knew personally. The worker in a shoe factory in China has no knowledge or connection with the user of the shoes. The village tailor made clothes for those he knew personally, the garment worker in a factory in Indonesia has no knowledge or connection with the wearers of the garment. The factory produces an increase in efficiency, certainly, but it also leads to a more impersonal world, devoid of meaning.

Something similar takes place in the "service" industry.

Here we can actually take the non-remunerative work of a mother as our starting place. Hardly any service is so personal and intimate as the cooking, cleaning, and sewing a mother does in the home. The work of a wife and mother is a work of love that bears fruit in a happy husband and children who are well brought up, which means, among other things that they will be emotionally stable and secure, responsible and respectful of others. The old saying was, "A woman's work is never done". It is never done because it serves human lives that, in this world, are never complete.

The works of the "service industry," however, move first outside of the home, then outside of the village, becoming ever more remote, automatic, and impersonal to the point that phones are answered by computerized systems. To get to personal interaction in "customer service" one first has to penetrate various layers of automation designed more to prevent personal interaction than to foster it.

All this may seem anti-technological and indeed it is, not in the sense that technology is bad, but that we have simply followed along, without question, letting technology and the technological mindset take over our world. Technology, as such, is not bad, but the technological world is disordered in its removal from the natural, in its impersonality and meaninglessness.

Nevertheless, it is one thing to recognize a disorder and another to correct it. Destroying technology is no solution; our lives have literally become dependent upon technology. At least, we must stop celebrating technology, stop pursuing every new gadget, and we must start recognizing the power it has taken over our lives, and looking for ways to diminish that power. The computer must be a servant, not a master.

We must learn to prioritize and maximize work that is meaningful, personal, and truly human.

DIFFERENT KINDS OF WORK—A HIERARCHY OF DIGNITY

I have been writing about the dignity of work and the importance of work that is meaningful, personal, and truly human.

We can divide work broadly into two kinds: the making of things and the serving of persons. To that we can add then the maintenance of things made and the "maintenance of persons," e.g., health care.

The work is more personal the closer the worker is to the thing made or the server to the person served.

Machinery, automation, and computerization remove the worker more and more from the thing made, making work more efficient, but less personal. The same is true with the relation between those engaged in works of service and the person served.

There will always then be a tradeoff between efficiency and the personal quality of work. Nevertheless, a well-ordered society would, as much as possible, put the focus on the personal quality rather than the efficiency. The movement towards "globalization" is a movement towards efficiency at the expense of personal connection.

We can also reflect on the dignity of different types of work. This does not necessarily reflect remuneration, nor should it necessarily do so. That is especially so because it is impossible to put a price tag on "dignity."

First, we can point out that there are jobs that are immoral and shameful, like prostitution and drug dealing, even when the former is given the name "sex work" and the latter is legalized, as has happened with the marijuana industry. These "works" contribute neither to the well-being of persons, nor of society; quite the contrary. The legalized gambling industry pretty much falls in the same category, even when it is used to support public schools.

There is also a whole industry of souvenirs, knick-knacks, and curiosities, that have very little real artistic value. The entertainment and recreation industries certainly serve legitimate purpose, but recreation and entertainment certainly are not and should not be the primary goals of human life. Unfortunately, lacking any shared vision of a higher good, these industries have taken on a vastly disproportionate role in human life.

One problem with free-market economic theory is that that so long as money is exchanged between employer and employee, between buyer and seller, the economy is functioning and there is really no way to distinguish economic activity that really contributes something to society in terms of product or service and that which either does not contribute, or worse erodes and corrupts. That does not mean that free-market economic theory is flawed, just that it is limited. Unfortunately, no one seems to have any idea as to how a free market can properly be guided and directed without being suppressed.

In 1991, after the collapse of Soviet Communism, St. John Paul II wrote a social encyclical *Centesimus Annus* (*CA*) commemorating the 100th anniversary of Pope Leo XIII's foundational social encyclical, *Rerum Novarum*.

He observes therein that Marxism failed because of its intrinsic contradictions. He does not, however, give an unqualified endorsement of capitalism, though he does recognize the importance of "an economic system which recognizes the fundamental and positive role of business, the market, private property and the resulting responsibility for the means of production, as well as free human creativity in the economic sector."[10] But such a system must be "circumscribed within a strong juridical framework which places it at the service of human freedom in its totality." [11]One reason for this is the intrinsic limitation of markets. "There are collective and qualitative needs which cannot be satisfied by market mechanisms. There are important human needs which escape its logic. There are goods which by their very nature cannot and must not be bought or sold."[12] A mother's "work" is not and cannot be valued in market terms. Yet, it is both indispensable and altogether escapes the logic of the market. Paid "day-care" is never an adequate substitute.

In any case, continuing with our consideration of the dignity of different kinds of work, we can say that work derives its dignity from the contribution to the well-being, material and spiritual, of human persons and human society.

---

10   *CA*, 42
11   Ibid.
12   *CA*, 40

There is certainly a foundational dignity to those "essential" works that serve our material well-being: the production and distribution of food, shelter, and clothing; the maintenance of "infrastructure"; healthcare. It is also easier to put a "price-tag" on these kinds of work.

Work that serves the spiritual, intellectual, imaginative, and even emotional well-being of persons (e.g., priestly ministry, teaching, and the fine arts) possess a greater inherent dignity, but the more noble they are, the less they can be evaluated in monetary terms.

There is another realm of "work" that tends rather to be despised, because "quality" in this realm is very lacking. Nevertheless, these works possess a great inherent nobility and are indispensable for human social life—works of leadership, organization, and administration. At the highest level this is the work not of the "politician" or bureaucrat, but of the true "statesman."

In a just society, certainly all those who contribute by means of their work should also receive a sufficiency to meet their needs and that of those of their family. Nevertheless, while remuneration cannot be proportioned simply to the dignity of the work, it is essential that apart from market mechanisms there be a strong social and cultural recognition of the proper hierarchy of "value" or better "dignity."

All work is not equal in dignity, nevertheless St. Joseph always reminds us of the dignity that comes from the workman himself.

THE DIGNITY OF THE WORKMAN VS. THE DIGNITY OF THE WORK

There are types of work that are downright shameful, types of work that are pretty meaningless, and there are types of work that are, to a greater or less degree, inherently worthwhile.

Such distinctions these days are often viewed as offensive. Some people even want to remove the shame attached to something like prostitution. Even as regards honest work it might be regarded as offensive to judge that work as a garbage man is less noble than work as a schoolteacher. We might hear the argument that picking up and disposing of the trash is "essential!" We could also observe that garbagemen are not likely to do any serious harm in doing their job, but some schoolteachers rather corrupt the minds of children than educate them.

Nevertheless, it is important to recognize that some kinds of work are not inherently worthwhile, while some kinds of work contribute in a greater or less degree to the common good of the society. That which serves the common good more directly and on a higher level is inherently more noble.

The cultural recognition of the true dignity of different kinds of work educates the populace (and especially the children) to recognize and judge not only between good and evil, but also between good and better. Refusal to recognize a true hierarchy of value falsifies the perception of good and evil, good and better. That falsification is particularly destructive to the lives of children who begin to learn that everything is actually indifferent and meaningless.

Nevertheless, I have already mentioned St. Joseph, the carpenter, who engaged in honest work that contributed to the good of others and enabled him to provide for the Holy Family.

If we set that work of carpentry in St. Joseph's own time and place, it certainly did not rank as high as being a rabbi or a synagogue official. It would not have been as esteemed as a merchant or a landowner or an administrator. It would have been more esteemed than the work of a shepherd, or of a hired hand. For all that, St. Joseph was more noble in his person than any man or woman who ever lived, except his wife and the child that was entrusted to his care. He was not dignified by his work, but rather he dignified his work by the nobility of his character.

Contrariwise, some people are dignified by a work or an office of which they are not worthy; it is an empty dignity. Others, we could say, fill and even exceed the dignity of their work or office. So, it is much better for a person to impart the dignity of his moral character to his work or office, than to receive honor on account of a work or office for which he is inadequate.

Returning to the teacher and the garbageman: teaching is a more noble occupation than picking up garbage, but it is better to be an honest, hardworking, garbageman than a lazy, dull minded, ineffectual teacher.

If, however, we consider that different kinds of work possess a hierarchy of dignity dependent on their relation to the common good, we discover also an inherent inequality of social order. We also know that someone who is inherently suited to a more noble task, will find himself engaged in a lower place, while someone most unsuited will be found in a position of dignity, authority, and power. St. Joseph would have been more suited to sit on the throne in Jerusalem than the murderer Herod; indeed St. Joseph, the son of David, even had a better right to the throne. While St. Joseph was grieved by the evil rule of Herod, he was not at all distressed at being deprived of the throne but was content with his humble role.

Still this recognition of the more noble and less noble within the social order raises the question of privilege and equality. These days it seems that privilege is regarded simply as a bad thing; the implication is that privilege is inherently unjust, contrary to the equality that should hold among the different members of society.

We need to look into that matter more closely.

4
Equality and Human Dignity

EQUALITY OF RIGHTS VS. EQUALITY OF RESULTS

I have been writing about the dignity of the workman in comparison to the dignity of the work done, noting that sometimes the workman dignifies the work by the nobility of his character, but sometimes, a noble work bestows an undeserved dignity upon an unworthy workman.

At the same time, I highlighted the importance of the cultural recognition of the differing degrees of dignity inherent in different kinds of work or different offices, determined by their relation to the common good. Through a correct estimation of the dignity of different kinds of work (and the shameful character of some forms of work) a culture fulfills its educative purpose, forming its members, especially the children, in a right understanding of good and evil, and also good and better. Without this accepted hierarchy of value, all work tends to become meaningless, valued only in monetary terms.

Nevertheless, the recognition of such a hierarchy of value is very much contrary to the deeply ingrained sense of equality that characterizes our contemporary culture. This is further exacerbated because our culture of slogans and memes discourages serious reflection (which takes time and effort), masks the different senses of equality, and thereby allows the inculcation of one particular meaning of equality in a rather deceptive fashion.

Recently, I observed one prominent public figure criticizing another prominent public figure for undermining or denying "equal rights under the law," which is an essential characteristic of American democracy. The critic failed to realize, however, that what was at issue and what is being promoted today under the title of "equality" is usually "equality of results," which is a different matter altogether.

Equal rights under the law actually allows a place for privilege and hierarchy; equality of results does not. Unfortunately, people want results, even if that means bypassing law with its limitations.

Let me give examples from a contemporary debate that exhibit that dissatisfaction with the limitations of equal rights under the law. One of those rights is the right to face one's accuser in a jury trial, which is guaranteed by the 5th and 6th amendments of the Bill of Rights.

This poses a problem in rape cases because facing the rapist can re-traumatize the victim. As a result, there have been all sorts of efforts to abridge the requirements of due process in order to protect the victim. This has taken an even more extreme turn on college campuses in the matter of any form of sexual harassment (a vague term, lacking in definition) in which there has been practically no due process at all for a man accused of sexual harassment in a college environment. He might have his good name besmirched, be subject to school discipline, lose a scholarship, or even be expelled from the school, with little possibility of defending himself.

The underlying agenda issue here is not really rape or sexual harassment, but equality of results. The desired result is the advancement of women—who are particularly vulnerable in the matter of rape—to a level of equality with men in the economic and political spheres.

As for rape, the woman would be better protected not by laws that circumvent due process, but a culture of sexual discipline and monogamous, indissoluble marriage (as compared to the sexual promiscuity promoted on every side) that truly honors women as women. Law cannot prevent rape, not even by sidestepping due process, but culture can make it nearly unthinkable.

Something similar is involved with the BLM movement. As far as I can tell blacks in this country have equal rights under the law. Indeed, in some ways they may have more than equal rights since the category of "hate crimes" can make things unequal in favor of blacks. Nevertheless, equal rights under the law is rather limited. The law has to be applied and it might often be applied by people who are in fact racist. There are laws against discrimination, but such laws can never root out all racists. There are various ways also that racists can work around the law.

Nevertheless, if we consider Irish-Americans, who were once a despised ethnic group, referred to as "micks," we can also see that equal rights under the law is sufficient for a group that suffers actual prejudice and discrimination, to establish themselves over time. Between 1860 and 1960, when the Irish-American John F. Kennedy was elected President, the Irish-Americans advanced in American society because of their religious faith, their social cohesion, their strong family life, and their strong work ethic.

Now, however, something like income inequality is seen as irrefutable evidence of "systemic racism." Equal rights under the law is no longer enough. Equal results, equal income, must be achieved. Those who possess wealth are seen as unfairly "privileged."

Really, though, what democracy should be offering is not the illusion of a classless society, but the opportunity to have a voice and the possibility of social and economic advancement. The real difference between a democratic society and a society with rigid class distinctions between nobility and commoner is that the classes are permeable rather than fixed, movement both up and down is easier.

EQUAL OPPORTUNITY AND PRIVILEGE

I observed that at the heart of American democracy is the promise of equal rights under the law, which provides for "equal opportunity," especially for social, economic, and political advancement. This is very different from "equality of results."

Equal rights under the law does not deny the possibility of different social or economic classes, nor the privilege that comes with some sort of class differentiation, but would make those classes less rigid and more permeable so that ambitious members of the lower classes have the opportunity to advance their standing and will not be impeded by law from doing so.

This does not mean equal opportunity in the sense that everyone has the same opportunity to become rich, nor does it mean that everyone has equal access to the opportunities available. The person who stands to inherit a million dollars has the privilege of a head start in terms of wealth, while those who receive a higher caliber education will have a greater awareness of various opportunities and more easily know how to take advantage of them.

Equal opportunity really is no more than a prohibition against unjust discrimination; it means that a black man and a white man applying for the same job should have the same opportunity to be hired. Neither should be excluded on account of his race. In that sense, equal opportunity is a consequence of equal rights under the law.

Equality of results, however, rejects in principle class differentiation and demands absolute equality (economic, social, and political) across the board, declaring that the lack of such equality can only be due to unjust discrimination. Equality of results would mean that everyone, regardless of circumstances of birth and parentage, should, for example, have the same opportunity to attend Harvard University. That would finally mean the opportunity would even have to be independent of qualifications.

The idea of a classless society is a pure fiction and illusion that deceives the unwary by the offer of an appearance of justice and seduces the lazy by the offer of reward without merit. The truth is that, if we consider a purely monetary example, if tomorrow the world magically started anew on a basis of complete economic equality, within a year's time society would be once again divided between rich and poor.

So also, it will always be the case that there will be some who enter into this life in a more privileged condition, whether as regards health, or wealth, or access to education, or nationality, or social standing, or any other factor that bears upon the goods of this world.

Sometimes the privileged condition will be connected with some past injustice that cannot be corrected without doing more harm than good (even if there were a human being capable of making such a judgment); sometimes the privileged condition will be connected with an injustice that must be corrected (e.g., the parents are stripped of their ill-gotten gains and so the child who was born into a wealthy household ends up being raised in a poor household). In general, we can say the more remote the past injustice, the less connected it is to present privilege, and the less possibility there is of a present correction that would in any way be just.

Unfortunately, one of the weaknesses of democratic society is that it either gives an illusion of a classless society or it inculcates the idea that there should not be class differences. As a result, the "de facto" elites, feeling themselves equal to the lower classes, sense no obligation towards them. The elites in a democratic society tend to feel their privilege as due to them, rather than as a privilege bestowed upon them, a privilege that entails obligation. A truly aristocratic society inculcates the idea of "noblesse oblige" (nobility has its obligations) among the elite. Of course, human nature being what it is, aristocrats often take their privilege as their due and neglect their obligations. Nevertheless, beneath the influence of grace, true nobility is possible and has been lived, as evidenced by canonized saints among ancient royalty and nobility.

PRIVILEGE OF BIRTH: ATHEISM VS. DIVINE PROVIDENCE

There will be some who enter into this life in a more privileged condition, whether as regards health, or wealth, or access to education, or nationality, or social standing, or any other factor that bears upon the goods of this world. I have suggested that this is not inherently bad, even if sometimes a past injustice was involved. Indeed, that past injustice cannot automatically be regarded as the decisive factor.

Suppose a man acquires vast wealth through unjust means and then passes that wealth on to his heirs. Next, suppose that over the course of several generations his heirs increase that wealth (by just means) and make good use of that wealth for the upbuilding of society. So, after 100 years, for example, is all the good that has come through that wealth, wrought by people who did not directly share the injustice of their ancestor, to be characterized solely by the injustice of the ancestor? In the end, did it not result that men who were born into privilege on account of an injustice, nevertheless fulfilled well the responsibilities that came with their privilege? They acquitted themselves nobly, even if their forbear was a rascal and a criminal.

Of course, it can go the other way as well. One man, through hard work and honest industry amasses a fortune that he leaves to his children. After his death, though, his children, lacking in gratitude and judging their fortune to be their entitlement, end up either squandering their fortune or abusing the power that it brought them.

Such are the ups and downs of human life.

Now, one thing to observe here is that the atheist, who cannot rightly believe in any sort of providence nor even any benevolent "luck," must despair in the face of these inequalities. He can see in this type of inequality nothing but a sort of cruel impersonality. Actually, that is how an atheist, if he is logical, should see the world and life in general—cruelly impersonal, or impersonally cruel. Human life becomes nothing more than an unending game of "King of the Hill."

The problem goes even deeper. Consider that every single human being is individually, from an atheistic perspective, nothing more than a most improbable accident.

Without even considering the accident of human existence itself, the existence of an individual, say Winston Churchill, required the improbable accident that his parents met and united at the right time in the right circumstances so that of the father's countless sperm the one that would produce Winston fertilized the mother's ovum. Then between the time of his conception and the completion of his first year there were probably any number of close calls (many completely unknown to his parents) that could have put an end to little Winston. The same was true, by the way of Adolf Hitler. The same is true of each one of us. In our conception, birth, and survival, we are each the result of an extraordinary set of coincidences.

From the atheistic perspective the magnification of this improbability of our existence makes life all the more meaningless. Our faith, however, assures us not only that God exists, but also that he governs all things by his mighty, wise, and loving providence. This transforms all these accidental circumstances of our individual existence into carefully planned expressions of God's love, of which we are the personal beneficiaries.

The perspective of divine providence, however, introduces a new perspective on privilege, together with one great equalizer.

The worldly perspective of privilege prioritizes such things as economic and social standing. Since the goal of divine providence is not a person's temporal well-being, but eternal salvation, those are most truly privileged by birth who enter the world in circumstances that most equip them to recognize and respond to the goodness of God, revealed above all in the salvific work of Jesus Christ.

THE GREATEST OF PRIVILEGES: MARRIED PARENTS, THE CATHOLIC FAITH, DIVINE GRACE

The privilege of birth (and lack thereof) involves an extraordinary coincidence of countless accidents; each one of us, individually and impersonally, from the perspective of all created causality, is most improbable. For the atheist this thought is intolerable evidence of the utter meaningless of human life, for the believer it is like a kiss of divine love.

The most basic "privilege," one that shouldn't even really be a privilege, but appears today to be becoming more and more of a privilege, is that of being born of married parents who love one another. There is no greater natural gift that a child can have upon his entrance in the world and in the years of his youth.

One woman, one of seventeen children, put it this way, "The permanence of their marriage, our happy childhoods, and our eternal happiness were their main concerns. We knew and we felt it like a warm blanket or, at times, a hair shirt, or like the ground under our feet."

"The ground under our feet": the parent's marriage is the bedrock of a child's whole existence. In the measure that the parent's marriage is solid, the child receives a fundamental psychological stability that makes it easier for him to see things the way they are and to live in the real world with a vision of goodness and hope. The child receives a capacity to trust and from the capacity for trust comes a capacity to love.

Contrariwise, we see how easily the failures of parents, within marriage or without, leave their children deeply wounded, especially in their capacity to trust and to love; their lives easily become marked by fear and suspicion. Well, someone who is capable of trust and love is more capable of recognizing the goodness of God than someone who is inherently fearful and suspicious.

When it comes to the relationship to God, however, the greatest privilege of birth (or shortly thereafter) is baptism into the Catholic Church and instruction in the Catholic faith.

St. Thomas Aquinas speaking of the need for divine revelation affirms that it was necessary for God to make known to us certain truths that exceed the capacity of human reason (i.e., we could never, under any circumstance, figure them out for ourselves) precisely because he has destined us for the supernatural blessedness of eternal life, a goal that exceeds our natural capacity. Yet, even as far as those truths about God that human reason is capable of attaining, St. Thomas notes could "only be known by a few, and that after a long time, and with the admixture of many errors."[1]

The Catholic Church provides the faithful with all the truth that God wants us to know about himself and his plan of salvation, together with the fulness of the means necessary to attain salvation.

The greatest of privileges a child can receive is to be raised in the Catholic faith. It is a great privilege, but we must remember, with privilege comes responsibility. "Noblesse oblige": the royal status of the children of God carries with it the royal responsibilities of the children of God.

The Catholic faith is not a treasure to be hoarded, but an amazing gift that should be shared with as many as possible.

There is, however, a great equalizer, the grace of God, given to whom he wills, when he wills, in the measure he wills.

There are many who have the privilege of being born into a fine Catholic family, but never seem to amount to much in terms of the life of grace, whether because of their own failure to respond, or because the mysteries of the dispensation of God's grace we do not know.

On the other hand, God's grace has the power to touch and transform the lives of persons who enter the world in the most desperate of circumstances or who during the course of their life suffered the most horrific misfortunes. All other privileges are as nothing in comparison to the privilege of God's grace. St. Paul, who excelled in terms of the privileges of the Old Covenant, declared, *I consider everything as loss because of the supreme good of knowing Christ Jesus my Lord.*[2]

---

1   *ST, Ia, q. 1, a. 1*
2   Phil. 3:8

He also, in face of the mysteries of divine providence, exclaimed with admiration and praise that defies the atheist:

> O the depth of the riches and wisdom and knowledge of God! How unsearchable are his judgments and how inscrutable his ways! "For who has known the mind of the Lord, or who has been his counsellor?" "Or who has given a gift to him that he might be repaid?" For from him and through him and to him are all things. To him be glory and praise forever. Amen.[3]

THE FUNDAMENTAL DIGNITY OF THE HUMAN PERSON

I have spent some time writing about the place and dignity of work in the realm of social justice, that is in a just social order. Even without considering the remuneration that people receive for their work I observed that different kinds of work are not all equal as to their dignity and a rightly ordered society will honor different forms of work according to their true dignity.

That led to a discussion of the much-agitated question of equality, distinguishing between equality of rights as compared to equality of results. Justice requires some manner of equal rights, not equal results. Indeed, any social order, just or unjust, will necessarily involve some sort of class structure. That class structure will mean that members of the upper classes will enjoy some sort of privileges and, for those who are born into upper classes, there will even be privileges of birth.

This is not a bad thing but must be moderated by the ancient principle "noblesse oblige," nobility has its responsibilities, so do elites. There can be no social justice, in fact, except in the measure that the elites are aware of and fulfill their responsibilities. Social injustice results not from power and privilege, but from the abuse of power and privilege.

---

3   Rom. 11:33–36

Nevertheless, I pointed out that beyond all the privileges of social, economic, and political standing, the greatest privileges of all are actually those of being born of married parents, the gift of the Catholic faith, and the gift of divine grace.

Dignity, inequality, and privilege, all these concepts are interrelated and lead us to what is often cited as the most basic principle of Catholic social teaching: the dignity of the human person.

So far I have not directly addressed this issue, but it has been implied in everything that I have written.

Nevertheless, while the dignity of the human person is a fundamental principle of social justice, I don't think it is a proper starting place for an exposition of the subject matter. That is because the concept is rather abstract and is frequently bandied about in a careless and meaningless fashion so as to justify all manner of nonsense. Instead, by starting with the original order of Eden, I took as my starting point man in the most fundamental, concrete relationships that characterize his life, individually and socially: his relation to God, the interior order of his soul, the relation between man and woman in marriage, and his relation to the environment.

I have not said much about the interior order of the soul because while this is necessary for social justice, it does not directly bear upon human social order. I have, however, spoken about the foundational character of our social relationship to God, the right order of man and woman in marriage, and also work, through which man is in relation to the environment, though I have yet to speak directly to the impact of work on the environment.

We now have enough of a picture of the right order of human social life to say something in a meaningful fashion about the dignity of the human person. What we need to see is how human dignity is equal, how it is rightly unequal, how it can never be lost, and how it can be lost.

First, though, let me point out what I think is a

much-abused expression, "the sacredness of human life." The right understanding of the expression refers to man's being created by God and in his image.

Nevertheless, from a Catholic perspective, in which the natural, created world is subject to sin, I don't think it is good to speak about the inherent "sacredness" of human life. In the traditional Catholic vocabulary the word "sacred" is reserved for what belongs to the order of grace and redemption. Human life is not born sacred but needs to be sanctified through the sacrament of baptism. Baptism, through imparting of the indelible character, truly sets the baptized person apart, consecrates him to God, and makes him to be "sacred."

Nevertheless, every human person, through being created by God, in his image, possessing thereby a rational, human nature, possesses inherent dignity. The fundamental equal dignity of all men comes from their sharing in human nature, a rational nature, created in the image of God. That is a dignity that can never be lost.

That all men equally share in a rational nature does not mean that all men are equally and at all times capable of the exercise of reason. Nevertheless, from the moment of conception the human person, simply because he is human, possesses a rational nature, a nature that is capable of reasoned knowledge, and consequently capable also of free choice, even if due to time or other circumstances a particular person may be impeded from the exercise of reason and choice. The rational power is what makes man to be in the image of God, who freely created all things by the power of his word, the expression of the divine reason.

That is the fundamental dignity of the human person, which makes him responsible in the aforesaid relationships, towards God, towards himself, towards his fellows, and towards the world that has been entrusted to his care. That dignity cannot be lost, but there is another sort of dignity that depends upon the way he fulfills or fails to fulfill his responsibility.

THE GRADATIONS OF HUMAN DIGNITY: THE DEGRADATION OF VICE AND THE ELEVATION OF VIRTUE AND GRACE

I explained that fundamental human equality and dignity is found in our rational nature, which makes us to be in the image of God, in which we all share, and which makes us responsible in our relationships to God, ourselves, to others, and to the world around us. This dignity cannot be lost.

Nevertheless, we are personally responsible for what follows upon or what we build upon this fundamental dignity. In this respect we are by no means equal.

First, on the natural level there is the dignity of virtue and the degradation of vice.

Through the practice of virtue, we learn to use our humanity, shall we say, as it was meant to be used. Once practice produces a firmly established virtuous character, we possess the power to use our humanity rightly. That means directing our life, including our interior faculties of imagination and emotion, according to reason and truth, rather than simply following our impulses and passions. Established virtue increases the innate dignity of the human person, making the rational nature to shine forth with a special brilliance.

Contrariwise, vice enslaves a person to one or more disordered passions. The reason is darkened, especially as regards the truth about God and human life, and becomes chained to the service of passion. In the worst cases, the reason is so weakened that a person begins to live more by animal instinct. Vice does not altogether destroy the innate dignity of the person, but it most certainly obscures it. The light of reason is hidden beneath the bushel basket of passion.

To avoid misunderstanding, reason properly speaking is our window on reality; to live by reason means living in the real world. The cold calculating genius, who pursues his own agenda, is akin to the madman in that he does not really live in the real world, but rather refashions whatever small part of the world he can control, to suit his own purposes.

To live in reality a person must have at least some vision of the whole, including God, the Creator of the whole; partial vision, when it is taken for the whole, radically distorts the understanding of reality, cutting the person off from reality.

Because of the inheritance of sin, true natural virtue is nearly impossible to attain, though some people who inherit a good disposition and felicitous circumstances might make some show of it.

There is, however, another level of dignity that belongs to the order of grace, the dignity of the children of God. Here there is the dignity of the baptismal character, the dignity of sanctifying grace (received in baptism), and the dignity of a life of actual faith, hope, and charity, a life of holiness.

In the beginning God created man in his image *and likeness*. The "likeness" adds to the image, elevates the image, making the man to share in the very life and nature of God. This sharing in the life and nature of God is called sanctifying grace, which was lost to the human race through the sin of Adam, won back for us by the death of Christ on the Cross, and given to us personally through faith (at least the faith of the Church and of the parents and godparents) and baptism.[4]

Sanctifying grace can be lost again through sin and regained through confession, but the baptismal character, which marks us as belonging to Christ, can never be lost and, so long as we remain in this life, is a perpetual call to remember the height from which we have fallen and so return to God.[5]

As the life of natural virtue makes the light of reason to shine forth in a human life, the life of holiness makes the splendor of reason, raised up to share the dignity of the children of God, to shine forth.

---

4   CCC 396–406, 1987–1995
5   Cf. Rev. 2:4–5

The baptized Christian who is living in sin, but who still retains the virtues of faith and hope, retains thereby something of the dignity of the children of God. The heretic or apostate has extinguished that light altogether. Even whatever natural virtue he possesses is debased by being turned against Christ.

The supreme dignity of the human person is that of the saints in heaven where *star differs from star in glory* depending upon the degree of holiness attained during this life.[6] Supreme above the saints is the perfect beauty of the Blessed Virgin Mary, the Immaculate Mother of God.

The dignity of creation in the image of God is a pure gift received that can never be lost; the dignity of sanctifying grace is an incomparably greater gift, but it can be lost; the dignity of heavenly glory is the supreme gift, which can never be lost. Heavenly glory is also the crown of merit, rooted in the gift of grace. Remember: *noblesse oblige*; dignity brings responsibility; responsibility leads to the true joy of loving service.

Vice diminishes the natural dignity of human nature and mortal sin loses the supernatural dignity of grace. Mortal sin violates and pollutes the temple of God within the soul.

Vice and mortal sin merit punishment, whether in this life or in the next, whether by the judgment of man or of God, whether remedial or eternal.

---

6 Cf. 1 Cor. 15:41

5

Universal Destination of Goods, Private Property, and the Environment

MAN'S DOMINION OVER CREATION: THE UNIVERSAL DESTINATION OF GOODS AND PRIVATE PROPERTY

We have considered social justice, seen through the eyes of faith, built around the pillars of the right worship of God, through the Mass, on the Lord's Day, and the life of marriage and family. After that we considered the place of work, the dignity of the worker and the dignity of work. This led to a discussion of the dignity of the human person, the fundamental equality in the dignity of human nature, the gradations of dignity in the order of nature and of grace, the legitimacy and role of privilege, and the supreme privilege of divine grace, which is brought to fulfillment in the glory of eternal life.

It remains to say something about the relation of work to property and the environment, or the relation of man, through work, to property and the environment.

At the root of this discussion, we must always turn to the original creation of man and the words of God:

> Be fertile and multiply; fill the earth and subdue it. Have dominion over the fish of the sea, the birds of the air, and all living things that move on the earth. God also said: See, I give you every seed-bearing plant all over the earth and every tree that has seed-bearing fruit on it to be your food. [1]

---

1   Gen. 1:28–29

This passage should be read also in the light of the words: *The Lord God then took the man and settled him in the garden of Eden, to cultivate it and care for it.*[2]

If we simply read the words "fill the earth and subdue it" we might make the mistake of seeing the earth purely as raw material for human industry, to be used according to our will and good pleasure. Our dominion over the living things would, in turn, mean the dominion of a master over a slave, free to dispose of the slave as he wills. Nevertheless, the expression from the second chapter, *to cultivate it and care for it*, clearly shows that human dominion over creation is beneath God, according to the laws of God, respecting the nature of what is "cultivated and cared for." Our dominion is a dominion that a steward exercises beneath his Lord.

So, while on the one hand the earth is to provide us with what we need to sustain our life, on the other we are to care for the earth, bringing it to its own perfection. The earth is not perfect in its "wild" state, coming forth from the hand of the Creator, because the Creator did not make the earth to be perfect without man. The earth needs man to bring it to perfection through "cultivation and care." In some way, the perfect earth will be the "domesticated" earth. Or the perfection will consist in the wild part being ordered to the domesticated part, so that the whole receives its perfection through the part that is domesticated.

Nevertheless, proper domestication would not mean leveling and killing everything in order to pave it over with concrete or asphalt but would rather mean a harmonious development of nature. That, at least, would have happened had man gone forth from Eden, to fulfill his mission, without having rebelled against God and fallen into sin.

Note that by seeing the whole earth as given to our first parents by God, we see also that the earth was given to the whole of humanity to provide for human need. This gives rise to what has been called "the principle of the universal destination of goods". Vatican II stated: "God destined the

---

2   Gen. 2:15

earth and all it contains for all men and all peoples so that all created things would be shared fairly by all mankind under the guidance of justice tempered by charity."[3]

We can get ahead of ourselves a little bit here and observe that this principle implies the need for a legal and juridic order to organize and govern man's use of the earth. This would have been the case even had Adam not sinned. The order of justice, however, by itself will not work unless "tempered by charity." Love, specifically the love of God, must motivate the practice of justice, the making and obeying of laws. This leads us back to our first principle of worship of God, because charity is impossible without grace.

The earth is given to mankind as a whole, but its use will necessarily be divided among individuals, families, and groups. "Universal destination and utilization of goods do not mean that everything is at the disposal of each person or of all people, or that the same object may be useful or belong to each person or all people."[4]

Indeed, it is precisely through work, which transforms the earth, that the earth is appropriated to one or another person. *"By means of work and making use of the gift of intelligence, people are able to exercise dominion over the earth and make it a fitting home*: 'In this way, he makes part of the earth his own, precisely the part which he has acquired through work; *this is the origin of individual property.'"*[5]

To sum up, the stewardship of man over the physical world, established by work, involves two basic principles of Catholic social teaching: the universal destination of goods and private property. The three aforementioned quotes from important Church documents summarize these principles.

Allow me to bring in what might be called a sort of "methodological" observation.

Modern thought tends to be extremely abstract, meaning that it pretends to view reality from a so-called

3   *GS, 69*
4   *Compendium of the Social Doctrine of the Church,* 173
5   Ibid., 176; Citing Pope John Paul II, *CA,* 31

"objective standpoint," as though from the outside. When this mentality governs the practical realm, especially as it pertains to the political and social life of man, it can be extremely dangerous and destructive.

Looking at reality from the outside, always an illusion, looks at reality as an object that man can manipulate and control at will, rather like a machine. It means looking at the "machinery" of the world and how we can tinker with it and even refashion it. Indeed, in relation to the environment this gives rise to the exploitative mentality; the question of whether or not something should be done takes second place as to whether or not it is in our power to do it. The same mentality, when applied to human life itself, becomes even more dangerous and destructive. Human nature becomes something to be tinkered with and refashioned at will by those who hold political, economic, or scientific power; these, usurping the place of God, refashion the lives of the less powerful. It is the cruelest tyranny of all; this is the mentality that has given rise to all the totalitarianisms of the modern world.

With respect to the relation between the universal destination of goods and private property the temptation is to look at the actual situation, see that goods are inequitably distributed and seek to invent mechanisms that will redistribute the goods in a more equitable fashion. At best, the mechanisms are artificial, having little regard for human nature and the actual circumstances of human life. Indeed, human life becomes subordinated to an ideal goal of mathematical redistribution. This, we could say, is the fundamental economic error of the various forms of socialism.

What is needed is a more organic consideration of how through human work the earth has been both naturally and historically apportioned to different individuals and groups. This perspective views man within his natural position in the order of creation. This in turn will allow a more realistic evaluation of both the just and the unjust in the distribution of the goods of the earth.

In the Acts of the Apostles we hear St. Paul telling the people of Athens that God "made of one, all mankind, to dwell upon the whole face of the earth, determining appointed times, and the limits of their habitation."[6] The appointed times seem to bear on the rise and fall of kingdoms and civilizations, while the limits of their habitation would refer to the different territories of the nations and peoples.

With Adam and Eve humanity begins with a family. That family multiplies to many families who then begin to spread out over all the earth, separating into different tribes and tongues, peoples and nations.[7] In part that is simply the natural process of the growth of the human race. Nevertheless, we learn in Genesis—in the story of the tower of Babel—that in part it results also from human rebellion and sin. The separation becomes a separation of misunderstanding and hostility. Christ's coming, in part, had the purpose of overcoming not the distinction of tribe, tongue, people, and nation, but of overcoming the hostility.

What actually results are different manners of apportioning care for the earth, together with different customs and juridical frameworks, arising from the historical expansion of man over the face of the earth, together with the conflicts that have arisen in the process. It is a process in which the just and unjust have been mixed together like the weeds and wheat in the parable.[8]

Always, in that appropriation of the land, human labor is involved.

UNIVERSAL DESTINATION OF GOODS AND PRIVATE PROPERTY IN PRACTICE

While God intended the earth to serve the needs of all men, since the earth only yields its fruits (literal and metaphorical) through human work, the earth has been

---

6   Acts 17:26
7   Cf. Rev. 5:9
8   Cf. Matt. 13:24–30,36–43

historically parceled out among individuals, families, and other groups as mankind fulfilled the Lord's command *to fill the earth and subdue it.* This has resulted in different customary and legal arrangements according to different historical circumstances. At the base of this distribution of the earth there is a fundamental order of justice found in the appropriation through different kinds of work, but the fundamental order of justice has been scarred by countless historical injustices arising from human sin.

The historical parceling out of the earth, though marked by human sin, has also been guided by divine providence. It has started with the growth of families into clans and tribes, and moved to the building up of kingdoms and nations, which during the course of history have risen to power, maintaining within their realms a certain order of distribution, and in turn fallen from power, giving way to new kingdoms and nations.

Modern economic theories, and this is especially true of Marxism, by failing to grasp the order of justice and divine providence in the organic development of kingdoms and nations, start with the evidence of present injustice and seek to overturn the existing order, imposing on it an abstract, artificial, purely man-made order of justice. It is as though a doctor, faced with a sick patient, thought the best way to treat the patient would be to kill him and replace him with a robot.

We might say that just as sickness presupposes an underlying health, so injustice presupposes an underlying order of justice. A true doctor does not impose health on a patient but works so that the underlying health that belongs to human nature, is able to come forth and over-come the sickness. So also, a true statesman, would not impose justice on a society, but would work to strengthen the underlying justice that is present, enabling it to wax strong and expel the injustice.

Nevertheless, before we get into the role of the states-man, or of government and law, it is necessary to continue further on the relation between work and property and the related theme of work and the environment.

I will try to apply the principles, illustrating them in relation to the settlement of the Pacific Northwest. First, I have to acknowledge that I am not an expert in this area in any way, so I am only making some observations and raising some questions. This enters into very controversial territory, but I am in no way making absolute claims, nor pretending to judge the matter. More than anything I am simply trying to illustrate the general principles in relation to work and the acquisition of property. Nevertheless, illustrating these principles in relation to a familiar historical development that bears on our life today will inevitably raise questions and present a perspective that is far from the usual and even farther from being politically correct.

So, in the first place, if we set aside for a moment the Native American claims to the land, from the perspective of the United States of America, the notion of "homesteading" made great sense and is deeply rooted in the natural order of human life.

First of all, homesteading shows us that the land itself is really the primary and most fundamental sort of "property." Next, by allowing someone to lay claim to land that was seen as unused, precisely by settling and making use of the land, homesteading followed the natural manner of appropriating land by way of work. The homesteader, by his work, appropriated the land to himself and his family. Private property is first of all ordered to the sustenance of families and the acquisition of larger holdings needs also to be justified in relation to the good of families. Further, raising crops or running cattle on the land the homesteader not only sustained himself, but also provided a good that would benefit others as well. In this way, the use of the land as private property returns to the good of many.

WORK AND THE CARE OF THE EARTH

But what about the Native Americans? Didn't homesteading fail to recognize the prior rights of the Native

Americans? Didn't it involve stealing the land from them? That is what certain signs displayed at the Portland "protests" have claimed.

I would suggest that the matter really is not quite so simple. It is necessary to distinguish the fact of appropriating the land from how the Native Americans and their prior claims were treated. In this regard there is a very important fact that is rarely considered, at least not presently: the land was underused by the Native Americans; the current population in Oregon, even east of the Cascades, away from the big cities, shows this.

The whole tragedy of the settling of the American west involves the conflict between large populations moving into and appropriating underused land, and the small population that was already there, whose claims were neglected and who were generally treated in a despicable and unjust manner. It would seem to me that the common destination of the goods of the earth was what justified the settling of the land by the "white man." That was not, in principle wrong. What was wrong was the way the Native Americans were treated in the process.[9]

Of course, that raises another question: the more extreme environmentalist will deny that the land was underused by the Indians. Rather, they will condemn the "white man" not only for his unjust treatment of the Indians, but also for plundering and ruining the land. This leads to the question of work and the environment.

The more extreme environmentalists are very anti-human as they see man not as part of the created universe, but as an alien being upon the planet earth, even worse a predatory being at that. I came across this on the Internet: "Coronavirus is the earth's vaccine; we're the virus."

---

9   A good example of mistreatment is found in first entering into the Fort Laramie Treaty of 1868, which established the Great Sioux Reservation. Then when gold was discovered in the Black Hills, excepted forever from white settlement, the US reneged on the treaty. Sadly, the examples could be multiplied ad nauseam.

This is a far cry from the vision given us by Genesis in which man is commanded to fill the earth and subdue it. Of course, many environmentalists blame Christians because of the "subdue it," holding that the destruction of the environment in the industrial age is the fruit of a Christian drive to dominate the earth.

The exploitive character of the industrial revolution, however, came rather from the rejection of faith in Christ. As I already explained the dominion God gave man over the earth was not a dominion to use and abuse, but rather to "cultivate and care" for the earth:

> The earth is not perfect in its 'wild' state, coming forth from the hand of the Creator, because the Creator did not make the earth to be perfect without man. The earth needs man to bring it to perfection through "cultivation and care." In some way, the perfect earth will be the "domesticated" earth. Or the perfection will consist in the wild part being ordered to the domesticated part, so that the whole receives its perfection through the part that is domesticated.[10]

So, properly, man is part of the natural world, not a predator upon nature.

Of course, because of sin the dominion of man over the earth has often become abusive; the industrial revolution in particular let loose a particular culture of exploitation. Just as the problem was not the westward movement of the white man, but his exploitation of the Indian, the problem was not the growth of industry as such, but the spirit of domination and conquest that has driven it.

Human history is a patchwork of good and evil; at every level the 'wheat and weeds' to which Jesus referred in the parable are present.[11] All forms of modern utopianism simplify the matter by making facile arguments to put

10 See p. 152.
11 Cf. Matt. 13:24–30; 36–41

all the justice on one side and all the injustice on the other. Rather than recognizing the good in the inheritance received and trying to move forward in a good direction from there, wheat and weeds are pulled up together.

Still, the industrial revolution has changed the way man relates to the environment by means of his work, tending to make it more a relation of exploitation, rather than of cultivation and care. More needs to be said on this subject.

INDUSTRIAL REVOLUTION: LIGHT AND DARKNESS

I have lived in the Scranton, Pennsylvania area, in which the scars left by coal mining are still visible. I have lived in Steubenville, Ohio, which has not recovered from the pollution of the steel industry. I have also lived in the Franklin/Oil City region of Pennsylvania, the first part of the world to experience the modern oil boom. You can still find debris from the old oil rigs in the woods. Each of these places shows how industrialism came in, enriched an area for a time with a booming economy, and the cost of environmental degradation, then moved on to new territories, leaving a depressed economy[12] and the scars of the environmental damage.

Notice the role of high energy in each of these three areas: coal and oil of course have been the two principal energy sources driving the industrial revolution; the mass production of steel required massive amounts of energy.

For just a small example of the radical increase in energy needs: a four-cylinder automobile engine might be rated at 130 horsepower; that might be more horsepower than a Civil War cavalry troop!

A classic economic analysis reduced the sources of wealth to three: land, labor, and capital. Or we could express them more broadly as raw materials, energy used

---

12 This cycle of boom and bust tears apart the intergenerational strength of families because later generations, unable to find an adequate living in the land in which they grew up, move away seeking more prosperous conditions.

to transform those materials, and durable products (means of production) capable of being applied to the continued transformation of raw materials.

In a pre-industrial society, capital is less significant (a developed mine here, a mill there, a kiln there, a ship), while apart from the energy of human beings and draft animals, energy needs were fairly simple. Industrialization vastly expanded the need for raw materials, forms of energy that dwarf the contributions of animals and men, and extensive capital goods such as factories, warehouses, means of transportation and communication. As we well know, massive amounts of energy have become essential.

It was no longer human labor transforming a field to make it produce crops or shaping a piece of metal to make a cup or a sword, but the human manipulation of machines—machines which have acquired ever greater degrees of automation and more remote means of human control—that have changed the whole face of the earth.

We need to acknowledge the advances this has brought about, but also the dark side of the progress as well.

As for the advances: vastly improved health care, vastly reduced infant mortality, increased longevity, more abundant food. These advances have reached wide swaths of humanity such that in many regions even the poor enjoy luxuries and conveniences never dreamed of by kings of past ages; there are also large populations that continue to live in dire poverty and are vulnerable to devastating famines and also poor health and its attendants.

Note, I have not listed the advances in transportation, communication, computing, lighting, heating, and "climate control." While they are certainly conveniences, it is not at all clear what real betterment they have contributed to the human condition, except insofar as they have served improved health and nutrition. Notice also that I have not mentioned at all the advances in the weapons of war.

That leads us to the dark side of the industrial revolution. First, is the diminution of what is truly human in scale and its replacement by the machine; we have moved from the age of strong men and weak machines to the age of strong machines and weak men. The mechanistic and technological reality also has shaped the contraceptive mentality and the legalization of abortion, which have compromised the whole realm of advanced health care.

Second is the movement of the majority of the population from rural areas to massive, overcrowded cities. Technology already puts people at a remove from nature, cities remove them even further. I would say that separation from the rhythms of nature has a negative effect on the whole of human psychology.

Human work should transform the natural world, yes, but in a way that is consistent with the nature of things.

Third, the artificial world of industry and technology has introduced an insane, frenetic pace to human life. The pace of modern life works against contemplation and reflection. Instead it produces superficiality.

Often, I encounter praises of the modern world that declare something to the effect that in pre-industrial society the vast majority of humanity lived in abject poverty with a life span of about 35 years. That claim seems very suspect. Before the industrial revolution, infant mortality was high, but if a person survived infancy, then he had a good chance of a reasonably long life. The Psalms refer to the human life span as seventy years, or eighty for those who are strong.[13] One would think that during the course of 2500 years or so someone would have remarked on how far off the expectations were. Certainly, past ages were marked by a keen sense of the general tragedy of human life, but that should not be exaggerated. I think anyone who is truly familiar with the high Middle Ages (1100–1300 AD) will realize that the people of the time possessed a sort of joy that is often very lacking in our machine world.

Now someone might ask, "What is your point, Father? Surely you don't mean to suggest that we throw out all of

13 Ps. 90[89]:10

our modern advances and start living like our ancestors of three hundred years ago?"

THE PROBLEM OF CLIMATE CHANGE — NOT WHAT YOU THINK

No, that is not my point. In many ways, for better or for worse, we are stuck with the industrial/technological world we have built. Nevertheless, we need to stop being bound by the slavish way of thinking that continues to insist that things are better this way, that this has truly been progress, even if now we could hardly live without it.

Further, I have been writing about the relation between human work and the environment. It is impossible to do so without recognizing the way that industrialization has radically changed that relationship and that the change has not necessarily been for the better.

The whole environmental movement has, to one degree or another recognized this fact. The environmental movement has been born precisely as a reaction to the dark side of industrialization. Nevertheless, precisely because it lacks the overarching view that the Christian faith can offer, the movement as a whole has been flailing in the dark. It recognizes that there is a problem but does not altogether grasp the origins of the problem.

As far as I can tell the environmental movement tends to be driven by two basic views: there is the extreme of a neo-pagan rejection of the whole industrial enterprise, together with its scientific underpinnings; then there is the scientific study of eco-systems and biomes. In actuality there seems to be a fair bit of overlap between the two viewpoints; both viewpoints tend to reduce the whole of reality to the natural world. The neo-pagan view will likely see man as more of a predator, while the scientific view will focus on how man can harmonize with the environment and even harness the environment in "sustainable ways" for his own benefit. The neo-pagan view will tend towards attention getting movements of protest; the scientific view will propose systems of control.

Neo-paganism tends towards anarchy; science, as a ruling force, tends towards control. The more anarchy prevails, the more forced control becomes necessary.

We could consider this in relation to the question of climate-change. In this matter, I don't have sufficient knowledge or expertise to have a definite opinion one way or another, but I can see questions and problems.

First, I have two general questions: are we really capable of determining and achieving an ideal global temperature? Would it be wise to try?

I would suggest that the answer to these questions is "no," but at the same time, while it is not openly stated, I think that behind much of the climate-change movement there is a hidden presupposition that the answer is "yes." Truly, whether or not we can make an impact on the climate, only God can control it.

Next are two questions specific to global warming. If global warming is taking place will that, in the long run, be detrimental to human life or beneficial? If it is taking place and will be detrimental, is it actually in our power to do anything about it?

That last question is key, since I have never really encountered a serious argument about it being possible to do anything more than slow global warming. Even that would seem to require massive, coordinated government intervention—such as have taken place in response to the Covid pandemic—that puts immense amounts of power into the hands of politicians, bureaucrats, and experts whom we have little reason to trust. Even then we would have little assurance that the measures taken would work.

Just as we have seen the pandemic bring out the total-itarian tendencies in experts, governors, and mayors, the one sure thing about a serious campaign against global warming is that it would be a path to totalitarianism.

We have seen, during the pandemic, that a concerted effort on the part of government and media succeeded in instilling such a degree of panic in a large part of the population that they meekly surrendered their 1st amendment rights to religion and assembly, without any protest, without any legislative action, but merely accepting executive decrees. As for the right to free speech, increasingly the tech giants are insuring that dissenting voices will not be heard.

There can really be little doubt that the same government and media forces that have given us the Covid regime would like to establish a climate-control regime of similar urgency and proportions.

Even though global warming is regarded as a "social justice" issue, none of this really has to do with true social justice.

Science Cannot Get Us Out of the Mess We Made

The neo-pagan current of the environmental movement conveys a sense of urgency and passion. Nevertheless, this has not diminished the hold that the scientific mentality has on society. By "the scientific mentality" I really mean the mentality that looks to science as the ruling force in human life. The contemporary environmental problems are the result of the industrial and technological revolutions, driven by science, nevertheless people still look to science to provide us with a solution to the problem. Few people seem to realize that so many of the problems have come about precisely because the scientific view is always partial, always misses something.

Further, science, when applied to human life, easily tends towards totalitarianism. Faced with a problem, the scientific mentality looks for a solution. The machine is broken; x, y, and z are needed to fix it. The body is sick; x, y, and z are needed to fix it. Human society is sick; x, y, and z are needed to fix it.

Well, in the case of the body, the individual patient has the choice as to whether or not to follow the regime followed by his doctor. He might have good reason for not following the regime. The doctor is considering only one aspect of the patient's life, his health. The patient in making his decision should have in view a fuller consideration of his good, especially his eternal salvation.

Now, the expert, ruled by the scientific mentality, tries to diagnose the ills of society the way a doctor diagnoses a disease, but the expert's view of the good of society is always partial, just as the doctor's view of the human good is partial. Only a good doctor, at least, is usually more aware that his view is partial than the "expert" who would apply his solution to the whole of society.

Further, applying the expert view to the whole of society requires the obedience not just of a single individual, but of a whole population. If the ill is judged to be grave enough then the remedy is imposed by force. Then we arrive at the totalitarianism of the experts, who addressing a particular societal problem, without a vision of the whole human good, especially lacking a view of man's eternal destiny, try to fix society by force, the way one would fix a machine.

Of course, because the expert view is partial, there are aspects of human life he does not consider, but which nevertheless are real. So, the attempt to fix one problem causes a multitude of other problems. This is exactly the dynamic we have seen in the way in which health experts, who have the ear of governors and mayors—and sometimes the President—have sought to address the pandemic.

Now, if we go back to our basic principles of human social order, we need to recall the basic hierarchy. First the order of man beneath God, then the interior order of the soul, then the social order between human persons, beginning with the fundamental society of marriage, which gives rise to the family, and last of all the relation of man to the environment.

Global warming or not, the last relation is clearly out of whack. Nevertheless, environmental disorder is a result of the disorder in the previous relationships, going all the way back to the order of man beneath God. The disorder of the modern world historically involves a turning away from God in a drive to dominate nature so as to be independent of God: the scientific, industrial, and technological revolutions have all been put at the service of this rebellion against God.

Without healing the first disorder, the rebellion against God, there is not much hope of treating the last disorder (the environmental disorder), without causing even further, more serious disorders.

The disorders of "transhumanism," the melding of man and computer, are not just looming, they are already arriving. There are already workers with microchips, containing personal information, implanted in their hands.[14] Smart glasses literally reshape the way people see the world. The development of robotics not only involves a further stage of replacing human beings with machines but offers increasing possibilities for real life "six million dollar men," who effectively are part man, part machine. The transhumanist ambition includes producing a direct interface between the human brain and some sort of microcomputer implant. This they regard as progress, but it is progress without any vision of the nature of man and the purpose of human life.

So, we might say the real challenge before mankind at the moment is, "Can we turn back to God and also resolve the problems that the rebellion against God has led to, without losing the benefit of the progress of science and technology?" Or another way of putting the question would be, "Can soulless modernity, symbolized by the lifeless machine, acquire a Christian soul?"

With God all things are possible; without God, even the best intentions go awry.

---

14 https://www.technologyreview.com/2018/08/17/140994/this-company-embeds-microchips-in-its-employees-and-they-love-it/

6
Government and the Common Good

GOVERNMENT: THE PROBLEM WITH RIGHTS

The consideration of the environment, the radical proposals set forth to address the questionable agenda of "climate-change" activism, and the looming threat of transhumanism, with the totalitarian dangers this all entails, leads finally to the question of government and its proper role in the realization of social justice. Government should come at the end of these considerations because it does not make human social life, rather it presupposes and serves human social life.

In any case, it is a commonplace in our time, written in the Declaration of Independence, that governments exist for the protection of individual rights. There is a problem here that needs to be addressed.

The problem is this: the good of peaceful human society requires that these rights be limited in some way. Freedom of religion should not allow the practice of Satanism. Freedom of speech should not allow pornography. Freedom of assembly should not allow riots.

Our Constitution as such does not provide for any principle of limitation, though actual Supreme Court jurisprudence has given us a complex history of precedents that provide some such principles. I am by no means an expert in constitutional law, but I expect a serious study of precedents would uncover numerous contradictions of principles.

Still, contradictory or not, these principles must have come from somewhere? Where? In general, these principles have come from the culture that formed the minds and attitudes of the Justices themselves. That means that the Constitution effectively has been interpreted by unwritten cultural assumptions that stand outside the Constitution itself.

I would suggest that until about 1925 the unwritten cultural assumptions in the United States were largely governed by a sort of generic Protestant mentality and understanding of morality. 1925 is significant because it is the year of the famous "Scopes Monkey Trial" in Tennessee in which a teacher, John Thomas Scopes, was tried for teaching evolution in public school, contrary to a state statute. The case was argued by two of the most famous lawyers in the country, William Jennings Bryan and Clarence Darrow. Scopes was convicted and fined, but the conviction was overturned by the Tennessee Supreme Court on a technicality. The real significance of the trial, however, is that it firmly established the myth of the conflict between faith and science, while at the same time marked the beginning of the ascendancy of science over faith in American culture.

The decline of faith in public life became firmly established in two Supreme Court cases of the early 1960s. The first was the 1962 decision in *Engels v. Vitale*, which forbad the recitation of an official state-sponsored prayer in public school. The second was the 1963 decision in *Abington School District v. Schempp*, which forbad the recitation of the Lord's Prayer and the corporate reading of the Bible in public school. Those decisions effectively secularized American public life marking the transition from limiting and defining rights from a generic Protestant mentality to limiting and defining rights from the basis of a supposedly neutral secular mindset.

We can consider the practical effect of this change first in the realm of religion. The Mormon religion was persecuted in the United States, for which reason Brigham Young led the Mormons to the Salt Lake Valley of Utah in 1846. While he would be named Governor of the Utah territory, Utah was only admitted as a State when the

Mormons agreed to abandon the practice of polygamy. The Mormon experience shows how the Protestant cultural mentality effectively limited the practice of religious freedom.

The Protestant cultural mentality also led to the persecution and exclusion of Catholics and Jews. Though both groups succeeded in carving out a place for themselves in American life, that nevertheless came at a cost of compromise of principle. This was most manifest in the election of John F. Kennedy. The Protestant opposition to the Kennedy candidacy was so great that on September 12, 1960, less than two months before the election, Kennedy made a special address to the Greater Houston Ministerial Association effectively promising that there would never be a meeting between his faith and his public policy. The Kennedy promise lay the groundwork for numerous Catholic politicians to follow suit with the infamous declaration, "I am personally opposed to abortion, but I cannot impose my faith on the country."

Nevertheless, with the secular turn of the cultural mentality, the door has been opened to the religious practice of Scientology, Wicca, and Satanism. At the same time, Hinduism, Buddhism, and Islam, have all received widespread cultural acceptance to the point that adherents of each of these religions have been elected to the US Congress.

The secular turn of culture has opened the door for radical religious pluralism, while working to exclude the public influence of traditional forms of Christianity.

Another line of secular development has dealt with the realm of sexuality. There has been a stream of landmark decisions beginning with *Griswold v. Connecticut*. Based on a newly discovered "right to privacy" hidden in the 14th amendment, this 1965 decision protected the "right" of married couples to use contraception. This laid the groundwork for the much more famous *Roe v. Wade* decision of 1973 that recognized a right to abortion. The right to privacy was developed in *Planned Parenthood v. Casey* in 1992, which upheld *Roe v. Wade*. More significant was Justice Kennedy's enunciation of a principle of radical relativism: "At the heart of liberty is the right to define one's own concept of existence, of meaning, of the universe, and of the mystery of human life."[1]

This laid the groundwork for *Lawrence v. Texas* (2003) which struck down an anti-sodomy law in the state of Texas. This effectively overturned the 1986 decision of *Bower v. Hardwick* in which Chief Justice Warren Burger had written, "The proscriptions against sodomy have very 'ancient roots.' Decisions of individuals relating to homosexual conduct have been subject to state intervention throughout the history of Western civilization. Condemnation of those practices is firmly rooted in Judeo-Christian moral and ethical standards." In other words, in 1986 it was still possible to invoke "Judeo-Christian" moral tradition as a basis for a limitation on liberty, but in 2003 the Judeo-Christian standard was flat out rejected and replaced by Kennedy's principle of relativism. Finally, *Obergefell v. Hodges* (2015) recognized the "right" to same-sex "marriage."

All this has left us with a radical pluralism in American life. Still, there has to be some sort of principle by which liberty can be limited. The basic principle that is used for the limitation of liberty is the "harm principle": In other words, people should be free to do as they please, so long as they don't hurt anyone else.

The most basic problem with the "harm principle" is that "harm" itself needs to be defined. There is physical harm, but then there is also emotional and psychological harm. Why not then moral and spiritual harm? Finally, any definition of "harm" implies an understanding of the good, which is beyond the scope of science, but is very much within the scope of religion and philosophy. Nevertheless, the relativist principle of *Planned Parenthood*

---

1 *Planned Parenthood v. Casey*

v. Casey effectively excludes any common understanding of the good. So finally, the judgment of "harm" comes from the subjective view of the majority of the Supreme Court justices.

In the end we have a huge mess in which competing power interests compete first to control appointments to the Supreme Court, then to win over the Supreme Court in particular cases. Even if the Supreme Court "punts" (e.g., overturning *Roe v. Wade*) that would effectively only throw the ball back into the court of the legislatures.[2]

Here we meet with a fundamental limitation of democracy. Presupposing a general consensus about good and evil, democratic processes can serve well to address practical matters in light of that consensus. Nevertheless, democracy has never been a good way to resolve fundamental life questions; too much is at stake for a minority to accept the rule of the majority in these sorts of matters.

Today, the United States is radically divided precisely when it comes to fundamental life questions, but there is no way of publicly speaking about or addressing these sorts of questions. We only know how to talk about "practical matters." So the democratic process becomes a vicious battleground for opposing world views, fought out on the territory of concrete practical issues.

Where am I going with all of this? Basically, the point is that while some measure of private liberty is necessary for the good of public life, it cannot serve as the foundation for public life.

So, before we address the role of government in relation to social justice, we need to consider the nature and purpose of government more generally.

---

2   Since this writing, *Roe v. Wade*, has been overturned by *Dobbs v. Jackson*, but no real decision on abortion was made. The Supreme Court did indeed "punt." The case was decided on the limited matter of the relation between Federal and State power. It remains to be seen what the long-term ramifications of *Dobbs v. Jackson* will have on American jurisprudence.

TRUTH AS THE FOUNDATION OF JUST GOVERNMENT

The experience of the United States and the radical nature of the divisions that torment our pluralistic nation show that rights require a principle of limitation and that the sort of limitation that has been historically applied has proven inadequate.

We could put it this way: freedom of religion does not exist for its own sake, but that men might worship God; freedom of speech does not exist for its own sake, but that men might learn the truth and teach the truth; freedom of assembly does not exist for its own sake, but that men might work together to achieve what is good.

In the measure that right religion is known, where truth is known, where the good is known, that common knowledge will put just limits on rights. Deviations in matters of religion, speech, and assembly may be tolerated, but only insofar as they do not unduly interfere with the practice of right religion, the communication of the truth, and collaboration for the good. In this context, freedom of religion, speech, and assembly presuppose two things: first, that religion, truth, and the good must be freely adhered to; second, that as much as these things might be known, in this life they are always imperfectly known and imperfectly realized, so freedom in these matters is necessary for growth in perfection.

This, however, is not the modern basis for freedom of religion, speech, and assembly. Quite the contrary, the modern basis for these freedoms is despair of truth and fear of being dominated by the imposition of another's will.

I remember once talking to someone about these matters and the person replied: "Who's to say what is true?" A good question, because so long as it is only one person's assertion of what is true, then truth can only be an imposition by one person on another.

"Gaslighting" has recently become a very popular expression. The expression comes from a 1938 British play, "Gas Light". In the play the husband tries to convince his wife and others that his wife is insane. He slowly dims the lights in the home, while insisting that nothing has changed, in order to get her to doubt her own perception of reality.

The expression has become popular because there has been a lot of "gaslighting" going on, both in personal lives and in the realm of politics. The major news media and big tech have become specialists in gaslighting. In this world of "gaslighting," "spin," "fake news," and "alternative facts," one could well fear the imposition of another's 'truth'.

Nevertheless, without a common recognition of the truth, each person is left isolated in his private world. Without a common recognition of truth there is no standard of judgment and therefore no justice of any kind. Without a common recognition of truth, human life becomes a perpetual warfare of conflicting interests governed purely by the law of "survival of the fittest," or better "survival of the strongest."

So, we must not despair of truth, but seek to know the truth and grasp the criteria by which a common recognition of the truth can be attained.

Speaking here of the truth, there are three principal truths to which freedom of religion, speech, and assembly point us. The truth about God (freedom of speech), the truth about the right relationship to God (freedom of religion), and the truth about how God wants us to live our life and for what purpose (freedom of assembly).

These truths must be the basis of any healthy political life and any just government. These truths are the foundation for a true "rule of law." Anything else, however it is "colored," if it is called "democracy" or if it is called "communism" or if it is called "government of the people, by the people, and for the people," is nothing but the rule of the strongest. That means that, whoever is in charge, the common people will most surely end up with the short end of the stick.

TRUTH AND THE NEED FOR AUTHORITY

After arguing that "rights" is an inadequate foundation for just government, I argued instead that truth is the only adequate foundation. I then went a step further to point out that the three basic freedoms (freedom of religion, freedom of speech, and freedom of assembly) should serve the three basic truths that we need: the truth about God, the truth about the right relationship to God, and the truth about how God wants us to live our life and for what purpose.

Next, it is important to recognize the difficulty involved in attaining the truth. The ancient Greek philosopher, Plato, in his dialogue *Meno* addresses the question of what virtue is and whether or not it is teachable. In the process of the discussion he ends up making a distinction between knowledge and right opinion (the Greek expression would be "orthodoxia," "orthodoxy," which could also be translated as "right faith" or "right worship").

Knowledge, he says, is "tied down," secure because we know a thing by the light of our own reason. Right faith, or orthodoxy, is less secure, because we do not know it by the light of our own reason but receive it on authority. Nevertheless, he points out that right faith, which is easier to attain, is sufficient for right living. Of course, right faith depends on the reliability of the authority that we trust.

This now leads us to St. Thomas Aquinas. The very first question he addresses in his master work, his *Summa Theologiae*, he talks about the necessity of divine revelation. I am going to reverse the order of his arguments. He makes a secondary argument that divine revelation is needed even for those truths about God to which we can attain by the light of human reason (i.e., true knowledge is possible in their regard) because such truth "would only be known by a few, and that after a long time, and with the admixture of many errors. Whereas man's whole salvation, which is in God, depends upon the knowledge of this truth."[3]

---

3   *ST, Ia, q. 1, a. 1*

Here we can take "salvation" very generally to refer to human well-being, individually and socially. Without the truth about God that comes from God, we are lost.

Even more so, because as human beings it is proper for us to direct our thoughts and actions towards some goal or "end," but the "end," the supreme destiny for which God created us, exceeds the light of our reason, that is eternal life in the bosom of the Holy Trinity, the beatific vision. We could never know that goal to direct our life thither unless God made it known to us. [4]

The point is that to attain the truth we need about God, our relationship to him, and the right way to live, the most important truth, our reason is not sufficient, we need authority, we need the authority of God who reveals, and we need to trust that authority. That is the basis of "right faith" or "orthodoxy."

This, however, leads to another problem: since each one of us individually does not have direct communication with God, we need to recognize how the authority of divine revelation is made manifest in the world.

Here reason will have to come into play, but not so much a highly sophisticated reason of philosophers, as the common sense of the human race. We can put it this way: there are at least elements of truth that are universal and recognizable by their universality, through the whole of humanity and through the whole of history (so far as we can tell). If the truth of an expert or specialist does not fit with this universal experience of humanity, there is no particular reason to trust that expert. The human oddity and eccentricity of some "experts" tells against them.

Nevertheless, the first role of reason is not to figure things out by its own power, but to look for, recognize, and embrace the authoritative teacher of truth.

Actually, the life of our mind starts out with unquestioned authorities, the authority of our parents and the teachers of our childhood. There, however, comes a time

4   Ibid.

of questioning when those authorities need to be either confirmed or rejected; still the presumption should be in favor of the authority that governed our childhood, which should only be rejected in the measure that it has been shown wanting and is to be replaced by another proven authority. The way of self-sufficiency is the way of pride and destruction. This is the way the modern world has followed and we have now almost arrived at the point of destruction.

That path of destruction has left us with a unique problem: recent years, recent decades even, have seen such a wholesale assault on universal experience that people begin to doubt what is most obvious. For example, people seriously seem to think that a man can become a woman and vice-versa. In a time in which nothing can any longer be taken for granted, we need to take stock of the basics of human experience.

The Basics of Human Experience and Divine Revelation

Starting from the need for truth to serve as the foundation for just government, I went on to elaborate the need for some form of divine revelation to manifest that truth and make it sure. This also calls for some sort of authority, communicating and teaching that truth. This shows that the first role of human reason is not independently figuring things out on its own but recognizing and accepting true teaching authority. This recognition must be based upon a correlation between what is taught and universal human experience. Not my private experience, but what has been always and everywhere.

Unfortunately, the modern path which has rejected any authority except the authority of independent reason has led us nearly to the point of destruction in which even the basics have been obscured.

So, let us review some basics.

The first chapter of the book of Genesis describes a world of sky, sea, and earth, sun, moon, and stars, plants, fish, birds, land animals, and man, which everyone can readily recognize as the world in which we live, even if a person does not believe that God created this world, or that it developed as a superficial reading of Genesis appears to suggest. Everyone lives on the same earth, beneath the same sky, illumined by the same sun and moon, breathing the same air. The flora and fauna vary from place to place, but every place man lives has its own flora and fauna. Even despite the enormous variation, a great many share the same experience of different kinds of flora and fauna. We can also agree with Genesis in recognizing that all of this is good. Technology and industry has removed a great many from that experience, but has not obliterated it altogether—at least not yet.

Next, we all talk. That is truly a remarkable fact. We talk about the world in which we live, about human life in the world, about things and events. Further, despite all the misunderstanding that goes on, despite all the lies and deception, despite a great deal of plain old stupidity, we sometimes succeed in understanding one another; real communication does take place. Even more, I would dare say some level of communication is possible between any two persons on the planet, taken at random (even without a common language) if those two truly desire such communication. That means that while it has often happened that some people have denied the humanity of others, we are capable of recognizing each other's common humanity, and even more that we do actually have a common humanity.

By the same line of reasoning, our ability to read and understand works written in the past, even the distant past, shows that we share the same common humanity also with those distant ancestors.

There are other common human experiences: art and music, religion (which if it doesn't refer to God or gods, at least consists of a common way of making sense of reality and life, embodied not only in shared "beliefs," but shared practices and symbols), marriage (at least as some form of regulation of the sexual relations between men and women for the sake of providing for the offspring), burial, and some sort of "government" (even if nothing more than that of a tribal patriarch or council of elders) that oversees common life. There is also a common life-cycle (though it might be divided differently in different cultures) of birth, childhood, adolescence, adulthood, old age, followed by death.

Of course, eating and drinking are necessarily universal experiences, sexual copulation is normal, and everyone also experiences sickness, pain, and various forms of weakness.

We also have an experience of good and evil, by which I mean people doing good or bad things, some of which at least appear to be quite intentional.

People talk about all these things, sing about them, and portray them in art.

So any truth about God and human life, whether attained by reason or revealed by God must shed light on this whole gamut of human existence and be able to make sense of it.

Modern science does not do a very good job of making sense of anything; at best it takes these things for granted and shows us patterns in them that we might not have noticed otherwise. Sometimes these patterns can be turned to practical purposes for good or ill.

Words, however, have a remarkable capacity to reveal to us the reality and order of things. I used words to set forth the above summary of common human experience, including the experience of language, art, and music. Homer, the great poet of ancient Greece set it forth much more beautifully in his verbal description of the shield of Achilles.[5]

So, if we are going to look for God's revelation, we would most of all expect to find it given to us in words. More than anything else, we would expect God to speak to us in some way, shape, or form.

---

5   *Iliad*, Bk. XVIII

Lest we go too far afield from our purpose of understanding the role of government, if a government is to be anchored in truth, then it must appeal not to weak human reason, but to divine authority, manifested in some form of verbal revelation that accounts for the whole breadth of human experience.

CAESAR AND THE APOSTOLIC AUTHORITY OF THE CHURCH

Just government needs to be rooted in truth about God, man, and the purpose and destiny of human life. Nevertheless, weak human reason is insufficient to establish this truth, which must therefore be made firm by some sort of divine authority, manifested in a verbal revelation. For reason to recognize this revelation it will need to be able to recognize that the revelation of God is capable of making sense of the whole scope of human experience.

Either no such authority exists, or it is different for different people, or indeed there is such an authority and it is one for all of humanity, whether it is recognized as such or not. If no such authority exists, then government can only be the imposition of the will of the stronger; if it is different for different people, then there can be no unity between those different people, only the uneasy truce of a "co-existence." Only if there is one divine authority for all the world and for all peoples could there be any possibility of "unity in diversity."

The only real candidate for an "organization" possessing universal divine teaching authority is the Catholic Church under the Roman Pontiff. Recent Popes have at least downplayed the political relevance of their teaching authority. Indeed, the tendency has been to put the Church at the service of a world unity, a universal brotherhood, that lacks a religious foundation. This has been manifested in a special way by the Church's promotion of the United Nations. Indeed, the Church has presented herself as a champion of "human rights" only to see those "rights" hijacked and turned against her by a whole new set of "equality rights" that favor the LGBT movement.[6]

Now before I go any further let me insist on something of essential importance: I am not setting forth a proposal for the establishment of the Catholic religion in the United States or anywhere else. I have been writing, and still am writing, about social justice on a theoretical level as the right order of human society.

If what I am writing is true, then it sheds light on the disorder of our present society but does not have much to say as to how right order might be established. In any case, the establishment of the Catholic religion, in the United States or elsewhere, could not justly take place without the conversion of at least a substantial portion of the populace to the Catholic faith, indeed it could not justly take place unless the Catholic faith became the dominate social and cultural force in society. That would also require a tremendous renewal within the Church herself, including a clearing out of the widespread corruption both in faith and morals that has been poisoning the life of the Church.

In any case, let us now turn our attention to the great political Gospel, the words of Jesus: *Render to Caesar what belongs to Caesar, and to God what belongs to God.* (Matt. 22:21)

The words are evidently true and just, but their meaning might not be so obvious as we tend to think.

Truly the words do speak to the relation of Church and State because Caesar represents all civil authority, while the Church, the Roman Catholic Church, has been entrusted with the care of what belongs to God. We need to grasp that there is an authority, in the world, but not of the world, that has care for the things of God.

---

6   Mary Ann Glendon has documented the extensive influence Catholic thought had on the drafting of the UN's "Universal Declaration of Human Rights." The thought that went into the drafting, though, takes back-seat to the history of actual interpretation and practical application.

Before leaving this world, Jesus said to the Apostles:

> All authority in heaven and on earth has been
> given to me. Go, therefore, and make disciples of
> all nations, baptizing them in the name of the
> Father, and of the Son, and of the Holy Spirit,
> teaching them to observe all that I have com-
> manded you. And behold, I am with you always. [7]

Notice first that the authority of Christ the King has
no limits. While he was on earth, the man Jesus Christ
did not rule over anything and even submitted himself
to the unjust judgment of Caesar's representative, Pontius
Pilate. After he ascended into heaven, he entered into his
kingship and now rules the universe with the fulness of
his divine authority.

Next, notice that he delegates to his Apostles a definite mission, together with the authority needed to carry
out that mission. That mission is universal in its scope,
extending to all nations on earth and through the whole
duration of time until Christ's return in judgment. That
mission involves leading men to faith in Jesus Christ
through the proclamation of the Gospel (*make disciples*), giving them to share in the life of the Holy Trinity through
the sacrament of baptism, and teaching them the way of
life proper to the children of God.

This apostolic authority comes directly from Christ the
King, is subject to no human authority, but is answerable only to Christ himself. Just as all men are bound to
believe in Jesus Christ, all men are bound to obey the
apostolic authority. [8]

Yes, the authority can be abused and God will call to
judgment those who abuse the authority he entrusted
to them. Nevertheless, the abuse does not take away the
authority.

---

7   Matt. 28:18–20
8   This is the true import of Pope Boniface VIII's definition in
the famous Bull, *Unam Sanctam* (1302).

The presence in the world of the apostolic authority of the Church presents a real challenge to the authority of Caesar, especially because Caesar tends to think that his authority is supreme; we need to think hard about the implications of our Lord's words in order to grasp the right relation between the authority of Caesar, that is all civil authority, and the apostolic authority to care for what belongs to God.

First, our Lord's argument bears on paying tax to Caesar. The coin bears the image and inscription of Caesar, so he says, *Render to Caesar what belongs to Caesar*. He certainly did not mean that Caesar has a right to all our money but there is a lot of meaning contained in that coin.

The coin minted by Caesar makes possible peaceful economic exchange over a wide area. So, the coin really represents Caesar's responsibility for the maintenance of a peaceful temporal order that allows exchange to take place and human life to flourish. A wise Caesar would realize that peaceful economic exchange and the prosperity that it represents is not the goal of his rule, but the sign that he has been ruling well.

When the rule of Caesar fails, human society falls into anarchy while lawlessness and brigandage abound. Travel becomes dangerous and it is no longer safe to go outside at night. Where such anarchy abounds, virtue grows rare and exceedingly difficult.

Caesar's true goal, though, should be that his people be virtuous because without virtue human life cannot flourish. The cradle for virtue is a healthy marriage and family life; children being born to married parents and growing up beneath the watchful care of a loving father and mother. The Church is the teacher of virtue by her doctrine and through her sacraments provides the strength of the Holy Spirit, which makes true virtue possible, even on a large scale.

But what are the limits of Caesar's authority? It is contained in Jesus' question: *Whose image is this and whose inscription?* The economic order regulated by Caesar's authority bears his stamp. Taxes are the price of admission into the benefits of the economic order.

But let us take Jesus' question and ask, "Whose image and whose inscription do we find on the human soul?" We find the image of God, the Most Holy Trinity, engraved in the human powers of intellect and will, and we find the inscription of Jesus Christ, our Savior, marked on the souls of the baptized. The soul belongs to God and is cared for by Christ's Church.[9]

In a word the things that belong to Caesar belong to this passing world; the things that belong to God and are cared for by the Church relate to salvation of souls and eternal life. As the things of this world, which are used by the soul, need to be ordered to eternal life, so the things of Caesar need to be ordered to the things of God. Caesar himself possesses a soul that belongs to God; he must give his own soul to God and must at least respect that the souls of those subject to his rule belong first to God. Further, Caesar is not the mediator between God and man, Jesus Christ is. The Church is not subject to Caesar but to Jesus Christ.

What belongs to God? Human souls created for eternal life. How are souls given back to God? In the first place through divine worship. Moreover, worship must not be limited to private, personal worship, it must be corporate and public. Rightly Caesar in his role as Caesar, representing the people, must also take part.

Thus Pope Leo XIII taught:

> Nature and reason, which command every individual devoutly to worship God in holiness, because we belong to Him and must return to Him, since from Him we came, bind also the civil community by a like law. For, men living together

---

9   St. Augustine asked this very question and answered it in this fashion.

in society are under the power of God no less
than individuals are, and society, no less than
individuals, owes gratitude to God who gave it
being and maintains it and whose ever-bounteous
goodness enriches it with countless blessings.
Since, then, no one is allowed to be remiss in the
service due to God, and since the chief duty of
all men is to cling to religion in both in interior
affection and exterior work - not such religion
as they may have a preference for, but the religion which God enjoins, and which certain and
most clear marks show to be the only one true
religion—it is a public crime to act as though
there were no God.[10]

The first role of government then is to provide for, pro-
mote, and take part in right worship, so as to give to God
what belongs to God. When a government fails to honor
God it turns away from the foundation of its own authority
and tends to make itself the absolute source of authority.

This fits with my starting point for this whole examination of the matter, rooted in the teaching of Genesis 2,
that the first and most fundamental human relationship
is dependence upon God.

Still, seeing as how there is little likelihood of any
major government in the world honoring God according
to the truth of the Catholic religion, what is the point
of even discussing the matter?

First, it reveals the radical failing of modern government, precisely because God has been excluded; second,
it keeps us from an idealistic enthusiasm regarding governments and helps us take seriously the words of the
Psalmist *put not your trust in princes* (Ps 146:3);[11] third, it
gives us a realistic view of what can be accomplished in
contemporary politics (limitation of real evils, accomplish-
ment of limited goods, and carving out a space for the

10   *Immortale Dei*, 6
11   Ps 146[145]:3

freedom of religion). The more we realize how radically disordered our system of government is, the less we will be inclined to look to our government for the solution to problems, the more we will want to limit the role of godless government in human life.

In any case, we need next to turn our attention to the next basic principle of government: care for the common good.

THE COMMON GOOD

It is very important to grasp that the common good is a good in which everyone truly shares, thus it truly unites people.

A pie is not a common good because each person has his own exclusive part of the pie. What can be common is that we are all sitting in the same room together, enjoying being together and eating together.

The Holy Eucharist is the greatest common good in which we can share in this life because even though the "bread is broken," even though there are many hosts, we all partake of one and the same *Bread of Life*, Jesus Christ, the Son of God.

It will be helpful to consider some other simple ways in which we experience a real common good in ordinary life.

Players on a sports team share the common good of the one team. Their contribution is different; their reward is not identical; but all share in the good of the team; all suffer together in a loss, all rejoice together in a victory. The victory is the common good towards which all their common effort is directed.

A family also has a common good. We could call it "happiness," not the happiness that each one has apart, but precisely the unique happiness that comes from belonging to a "happy family." What makes for a happy family? Mutual love and living well together. Again, each member of the family has a different role to play, but each member shares in the happiness that comes from the well-being of the family.

So also a nation has a common good. We could say that a sign of the realization of the common good is found when there is a widespread sense of pride in belonging. The more Americans feel good about being American the more we can be sure that there is a real common good in which they are sharing. The more they feel downtrodden or humiliated precisely because they are American, the more we can be sure that the common good has not been attained. The more people feel like they truly belong, the more there is a common good in which they are sharing; the more people feel alienated and marginalized, the more evident that the common good is suffering. When the nation is deeply divided, they are evidently not united by the common good.

One caveat is in order: if the feeling good about being American, if the sense of belonging, is rooted in an illusion or a lie, then they have attained only to a deceptive and illusory common good. The attainment of a deceptive common good will become a source of division.

So we need to ask: in what consists the true common good of a nation? That will be the responsibility of good government, guiding the nation towards the true common good.

INADEQUATE CONCEPTIONS OF THE COMMON GOOD

Often, we can get at the truth by understanding the opposing error, so by considering false conceptions of the common good of the United States, we have made an advance towards understanding the true common good, for any nation.

One false conception of the common good is national power. Americans have often felt good about being the most powerful nation in the world. Yet, that would often be a good achieved at the expense of others. We like to feel that it has been a power in defense of others, in favor of freedom, in favor of democracy, or the like. There is certainly some truth to the reality, but also the reality has been more ambiguous.

The United States has not just exported democracy and liberty, but has exported abortion, contraception, pornography, and weapons of war.

Another false conception of the common good, connected to the first, is economic prosperity. Americans have felt good about belonging to a nation that has produced the most prosperous economy in the world, bringing the greatest material prosperity to the greatest number.

Unfortunately, this is most inadequate as a "common good," one that has given rise to great internal conflict and turmoil. Always there have been people, sometimes large numbers, who have been left out of that prosperity. It also reflects back on the good of national power, because the ugly fact is that our economic power has often involved the *de facto* economic exploitation of weaker nations.

There is also a third candidate for a common good that makes Americans feel good about themselves: our constitutional democracy; the oldest constitutional democracy in the world. It is also the root of the particular American sense of moral superiority.

Yet I have already touched implicitly on the weakness of this view of the common good. The basic rights that characterize our democracy, freedom of religion, freedom of speech, and freedom of assembly, need to be limited, but none of our constitutional democratic government provides a limiting principle. As I noted, originally the limiting principle came from the culture of a generic Protestant Christianity; more recently that has been replaced by a secular, relativistic culture whose supreme value seems to be absolute equality. The secular relativistic culture has roots that go back to the embrace of the "myth of progress" and the drive to "conquer nature," that was present also at the time of the American founding.

Now characteristic of Protestantism is the importance of the personal conscience standing immediately before God (which is true so far as it goes) that is beholden to no human authority (not quite so true). This harmonizes well

with American democracy conceived as a political system
in which all are political equals because they are equals
before God and which serves the ability of each one to
serve God according to his conscience. At least that was
the position of the American man as head of the family.

That leads us to the real hidden secret of much of the
success of the American republic: while the primacy of
personal conscience was supreme, at the same time there
was a *de facto* moral consensus, rooted in the same generic
Protestantism, rooted even in the Ten Commandments.

So, if we consider the traditional role of the American father of the family and of the morality of the Ten
Commandments in American life, the real key to American prosperity has been a healthy family life rooted in
fidelity to the Ten commandments. That has been the
real strength of the nation. The success of the democratic
system has been in making that possible.

At the same time, the individualism inherent in the Protestant American notion of conscience, together with the
absence of any moral principle written into the very framework of the republic, has been the undoing of the same.

Still, the common moral life sets us on the right track
to grasp what the common good of a nation should be.

THE COMMON GOOD AS "LIVING WELL TOGETHER"

The real strength of the United States, which has sometimes been served by the democratic system of government,
has been a strong family life rooted in the morality of
the Ten Commandments.

Of course, it was not just a matter of isolated families,
but families living together in neighborhoods, which were
part of larger networks of communities, all of which was
bound together by shared values and mutual support.

I wrote about the realization of the common good of a
family: "We could call it 'happiness,' not the happiness that
each one has apart, but precisely the unique happiness that
comes from belonging to a 'happy family'. What makes

for a happy family? Mutual love and living well together. Again, each member of the family has a different role to play, but each member shares in the happiness that comes from the well-being of the family."[12]

As we move from families, to neighborhoods, to larger communities, to the whole nation, we could expand on that view of the common good and speak of the "happy nation" characterized by citizens, members of families and neighborhoods, who by and large have good will one for another and who seek to support each other in living well together, not everyone in the same way or to the same degree, but each one according to his proper place in the whole fabric of the nation.

"Living well together" turns out to be the key to the common good. Yet living well together is only possible if there is a shared vision of "the good life."

Further, the national common good cannot be conceived simply in terms of the living well together of individual citizens because the well-being of those citizens is insep-arable from their belonging to the smaller communities of family and neighborhood, communities in which the members know each other personally.

Further, just as not every member of the family has an equal role, since the parents have authority over the children and the older children must help the parents in taking care of the younger children, the same is going to be true in neighborhoods, larger communities, and the whole nation. There will be leaders of different sorts and there will be people in positions of authority.

The key, though, is the shared vision of "the good life."

Again, American pluralism and individualism under-mines the common good on precisely the point of "shared vision." The pursuit of happiness becomes one thing for one person and another for another person. In the words of Justice Anthony Kennedy, speaking with the authority of the Supreme Court: "At the heart of liberty is the right

12   See p. 186.

to define one's own concept of existence, of meaning, of the universe, and of the mystery of human life."[13] That principle actually renders impossible the attainment of any true common good. Even worse, it renders the very notion of the common good unintelligible. It tells us that essentially, we have nothing at all in common.

If, however, we return to a consideration of the Ten Commandments, we can discover contained therein a teaching on the human good.

THE COMMON GOOD: A SHARED LIFE OF VIRTUE

The Ten Commandments give us a view of the human good that comes from God and is accessible to human reason.

Traditionally we speak of the "two tables" because Moses wrote the commandments on two stone tablets.[14] The first table contains the first three commandments which govern our relationship with God; the second table contains the remaining seven commandments, governing our relationship with our neighbor. Let us start with the second table.

The 4th Commandment (*Honor your father and mother*) points us to the good of our human origins, those from whom we have received life. It also points us to the good authority, the original source of authority on the human level, rooted in the gift of life, and the first human mediation of divine authority. It is the link between the two tables and makes possible life in community.

The 5th Commandment (*Thou shalt not kill*) points us to the good of human life, forbidding the taking of innocent human life. It is good to be alive as human beings. It is good for me, it is good for you, and it is good for everyone.

The 6th commandment (*Thou shalt not commit adultery*) points us to the good of human marriage, the first and most fundamental form of human society and, beneath God, the source of human life.

---

13   *Planned Parenthood v. Casey*
14   Cf. Exod. 34:1, 27–28

The 7th commandment (*Thou shalt not steal*) speaks to us of the good of property, which is above all necessary for the maintenance of the life of the family and the good order of the community, built up from a multitude of families.

The 8th commandment (*Though shalt not bear false witness against your neighbor*) speaks to us of the indispensable good of truth and trust for human society.

The 9th and 10th commandments (*Thou shalt not covet*) tells us of the need to master our desires, especially in service of the human goods of marriage and property.

We can sum this up: human life needs to be rooted in a generative authority that gives rise to a shared life, built on truth and trust, handed on from one generation to the next. You might say that it is all about collaboration in raising children, helping boys and girls to grow to become men and women, undertake marriages, and have families of their own.

Here, though, we enter into a very delicate matter. Adults don't like to be treated like children, but adults also need to continue growing; they too need guidance in life; they too need authority; they do not know everything.

The commandments teach virtue, which is the stable character whereby a person does not merely obey the commandments as an imposition from without, but truly desires, honors, cherishes, and acts according to the human goods revealed by the commandments. The adult typically needs ongoing guidance in the practice of virtue so as to grow in virtue.

Living well together, living the truly "good life," following the teaching of the Ten Commandments, means living a life of virtue, the joint cultivation of virtue, each one in accordance with his station in life, in service of the human good. So, we might say the first level of the common good is a shared life of virtue.

Still, hidden within that shared life of virtue is the common good of truth, which even more than virtue points us to God and the first table.

THE COMMON GOOD: A SHARED LIFE OF WORSHIP AND CONTEMPLATION

The recognition of the human good as something true, not just true for you or for me, or for ancient times or for modern times, or for Russians or for Americans, but for everyone, everywhere, simply because they are human beings implies the recognition that human nature has a definite reality, which fits within an intelligible order of the whole universe. All of that finally points to God as the Creator of that order; it points to God as an intelligent being who makes his will for man known, in a first and fundamental way, simply in the way he has created us and the world in which he has placed us.

That leads us to St. Thomas Aquinas' definition of "natural law" as "the way the rational creature participates in the eternal law."[15] The eternal law is nothing other than the plan of divine providence by which God governs the whole universe.[16] Sub-rational creation is governed by the eternal law in a purely passive manner. Animals neither obey nor disobey God. Rocks neither obey nor disobey God. They do not know the law by which they are governed. Men are capable, by the light of their mind, and even more by the light of divine revelation, of reading the "law" that God has written in the nature of things and freely and voluntarily obeying that law, or disobeying. By sharing in the eternal law, through the natural law, he shares in God's governance of himself, he is both ruled and ruling.

The principles of natural law are, in theory, accessible to human reason but, in point of fact, are readily obscured by human sin, especially by the blindness of particular cultures. That is true in a special way of the present time that has become divorced from the natural law and has also succeeded in institutionalizing the violation of all of the Ten Commandments.

15   *ST, Ia-IIae, q. 91, a. 2*
16   Cf. *ST, Ia-IIae. q. 91, a. 1*

So God's revelation not only is necessary to make known to us the mystery of the Holy Trinity and our supernatural destiny to be attained through Jesus Christ, the Son of God made man, crucified and risen, but even to make known to us the basic principles of the natural law.[17] Even the commandments of the first table, which bear on our relation to God, belong in some way to the natural law, though it is specified by divine revelation. Natural law, we can say, commands that God be worshipped. The commandments begin to specify that worship.

The 1st commandment (*I am the Lord your God, you shall not have other gods before me*) commands the worship of the one true God, creator of heaven and earth, and forbids worship of any creature. At the same time, the commandment sets this worship in the context of a covenant, through which he saves his people. In the Old Testament he is the God who led the people out of slavery in Egypt; in the New Testament, he leads us out of the slavery of sin and death through the death and resurrection of his Son, Jesus Christ.[18]

The 2nd commandment (*Thou shalt not take the name of the Lord in vain*) protects the good of the knowledge of God, which is manifest by his name. At the same time, it commands that we be always mindful of his presence and reality, since using his name in vain always implies a forgetfulness or denial of his presence and reality. The 2nd commandment teaches us the importance of the truth about God, while showing us that this truth is not abstract, but personal. God exists and he knows our inmost thoughts and desires.

The 3rd commandment (*Keep holy the Sabbath*—or in the Church *Keep holy the Lord's Day*) prescribes a determinate time to remember the work of God in creation and salvation, to give him thanks, and to worship him. It teaches us the primacy of contemplation, directing the

---

17   Cf. *ST*, Ia, *q.1, a.1;* Ia-IIae, *q. 100, a. 1*
18   Cf., Exod. 20:1

mind and heart towards God above all. By extension, the 3rd commandment also requires the setting aside of places, temples, dedicated to the worship of God.

The commandments of the first table, then, show us that the common good, "living well together," is achieved most of all when we turn together towards the supreme source of our being, our goodness, and our unity, the God who created us and redeems us, our first principle and supreme goal, in knowledge, worship, thanksgiving, and contemplation.

Without turning together towards God, the common good, even the shared life of virtue, falls apart. "Without the Creator the creature vanishes." [19]

Good government, then, must serve the truth about God and man contained in the Ten Commandments. In doing so, it will do its part in the realization of social justice.

---

19   *GS*, 36

CONCLUSION

The Interior Order and the Heavenly Jerusalem

I HAVE EXAMINED THE THEME OF social justice, the right ordering of human society, from the perspective of the original order of Eden: there was perfection and peace in four hierarchical orders, the order of man to God, the interior order of the individual human person, the social order that begins in the relation of male and female, and finally the order of man over the whole creation.

The basic foundation of my argument has been that the lost order needs to be restored starting from where it was broken, man's relation to God, which is achieved through the religion of Jesus Christ, namely the sacrifice of the Cross through which he won our redemption and its renewal in the holy sacrifice of the Mass. The holy sacrifice of the Mass is the stone that the builders of the modern world have rejected, which must become the cornerstone, not only for individuals but also for nations.

I have also considered the right order of male and female in marriage and the right order of man over creation in work and care for the environment. Finally, I had a few words about the role of the government in service of the common good, which is defined by this fourfold order.

I have not written anything directly about the interior order of the soul because that relates only indirectly to the right order of society. Nor have I answered the question, in the face of present social injustice, what must we do?

It has not been my intention really to answer that question. What I have written, I think sheds light on the vast scope of the problem, revealing that it is beyond human solution. That does not mean that people should just throw up their hands in despair, but it does mean that they should be realistic about what is possible, which is mostly opposing and limiting the evil. Indeed, we must not just lie down and let the tide of evil advance but do all in our power to oppose it, while working to carve out spaces in which the good can grow and flourish.

Further, the real answer to that question is intimately bound up with the right order of the soul. The exterior worship of God is necessary but not sufficient for social justice; social justice cannot be achieved except by men who have been purified interiorly and "rectified" through the right worship of God.

One current of the modern liturgical movement seems to have rightly apprehended that there is a connection between liturgy and social justice, but wrongly apprehended both the character of social justice and the manner of the connection. They thus tended to reduce the liturgy to being a pep-rally for progressive social activism. [1]

First of all, according to my argument the holy sacrifice of the Mass by itself is the cornerstone of all right social order. Further, participation in the sacrifice of the Mass is, we can say, the workshop in which the new man, the man of grace, the purified man, capable of living in accord with the standards of true social justice, is fashioned.

Returning to the prophecy of Isaiah and Micah,

> It shall come to pass in the latter days that the
> mountain of the house of the Lord shall be estab-
> lished as the highest of the mountains, and shall
> be raised above the hills; and all the nations shall
> flow to it, and many peoples shall come and say,
> 'Come, let us go up to the mountain of the Lord,

---

1   cf. Talk of Bishop Robert Vasa at the Sacred Liturgy Conference, Medford, Oregon, 2017

to the house of the God of Jacob; that he may
teach us his ways, and that we may walk in his
paths.' For out of Zion shall go the law, and the
word of the Lord from Jerusalem. [2]

The spiritual meaning of the "mountain of the house
of the Lord," of the "temple," of "Zion" and "Jerusalem" is
all realized in the holy sacrifice, is embodied in the altar
of a Catholic church. The instruction that leads to peace
is not just the word of God, not just the ecclesiastical
preaching, but also the very instruction of the sacrifice
in which we take part and the sacrament that we receive.

The new covenant is characterized by the law written upon the heart through the gift of the Holy Spirit.
Neither the asceticism of fasting and personal prayer
are sufficient. Nor is the practice of the works of mercy
sufficient, for someone to strip himself of the old man
and be clothed with the new. The law must be written
in his heart and this is the work of the Holy Spirit; this
comes about through the communication of grace and it
is the sacrament that is the efficacious means of grace.

This Pope Leo XIII in *Rerum Novarum* showed to be the
utterly unique contribution of the Church to social justice.

> The instruments which [the Church] employs
> are given to her by Jesus Christ himself for the
> very purpose of reaching the hearts of men, and
> derive their efficiency from God. They alone can
> reach the innermost heart and conscience, and
> bring men to act from a motive of duty, to control
> their passions and appetites, to love God and their
> fellow men with a love that is outstanding and of
> the highest degree and to break down courageously
> every barrier which blocks the way to virtue.[3]

The sacrament is the efficacious instrument of the
communication of grace, of the writing of the law upon

---

2   Isa. 2:2–3; Mic. 4:1–2
3   *RN, 26*

the heart, but the whole ritual of the Mass, rightly understood and executed, is meant to dispose the soul for the
reception of grace.

The whole rite of worship contributes, or should contribute, to the rectification of the soul. Yet, it must first
of all be worship, adoration; it must first of all be oriented to giving honor and glory to God, the Most Holy
Trinity. The holy sacrifice of the Mass is the cornerstone
of true social justice, but cannot be instrumentalized
for that purpose; it cannot be instrumentalized for any
purpose. Rather, men, who are focused on worshiping
God rightly, are transformed therein and, as a consequence, are rendered capable of living rightly. Even holy
communion, which unites the faithful in the Body of
Christ, is first of all focused not on that fraternal union,
much less on going out and serving the poor, but simply
on the union of the soul and her Lord. *For me it is good
to cleave to God.*[4]

I have written about social justice, starting from creation and the original order of holiness and justice found
in Eden, but the final and supreme light is the light
of the heavenly Jerusalem, *by its light nations shall walk.*[5]

The Lamb of God is found in the center of the heavenly Jerusalem, in place of the earthly Temple. (cf. Rev.
21:22) The same Lamb of God, in the sacrifice and the
sacrament is found at the heart of the Church on earth,
making the Church to be a sort of present "sacrament"
of the heavenly Jerusalem. The same Lamb of God is
received by the faithful in holy communion, making the
soul to be a sort of little Jerusalem.

In the measure that men whose souls have been transformed by grace transform the present world, they make
the social order of this present world to be also a sort
of reflection of the heavenly Jerusalem.

---

4   Ps. 73[72]:28
5   Rev. 21:24

In the order of Eden the foundation of social life was the relation of man and woman in marriage. In the heavenly Jerusalem, they *neither marry nor are given in marriage, for they cannot die any more, because they are equal to the angels and are sons of God, beings sons of the resurrection.*[6] The family of the heavenly city will be the family of Christ, those who in this life lived in accord with the word of God.[7]

The social order of the heavenly Jerusalem finds its reflection in this world in the monastic life. The life of contemplative monks and nuns, ordered around the sacred liturgy, the "work of God,"[8] bears witness to the reality of the heavenly Jerusalem, both as our goal and as present already within our midst.

First the Protestant Rebellion, then the French Revolution, sought to destroy the monastic life, precisely because it was deemed useless for this world. In the French Revolution active religious orders, engaged in works of mercy, fared better, because at least they were doing something. In truth, just as social justice requires the holy sacrifice of the Mass, it requires the monastic life. We need more monasteries and convents and more monks and nuns!

Transformation of the present world, according to the pattern of the heavenly Jerusalem is the goal, but we must keep in mind that, in this present world, we can achieve no more than a reflection, an image, of the heavenly Jerusalem. A man living in exile might want to order and decorate his house so that it will remind him of his native country. So life in this world should be "ordered and decorated" to remind us of our heavenly homeland. The final consummation, however, must come down from heaven from God when he makes all things new.[9]

---

6 Luke 20:35–36
7 Cf. Luke 8:21
8 *Rule of St. Benedict*
9 Rev. 21:2

The supreme and living embodiment of the reality of Jerusalem is found in the Blessed Virgin Mary, now assumed into heaven, reigning as Queen, our Mother and our Advocate. Her beauty is the beauty of Jerusalem; she brings solace, guidance, and help to our life in exile.

If I forget you Jerusalem, let my right hand wither! Let my tongue cleave to my palate, if I do not remember you, if I do not set Jerusalem above my highest joy. (Ps 137[136]:5-6)

FURTHER READING

Cavanaugh, William T., *The Myth of Religious Violence: Secular Ideology and the Roots of Modern Conflict*. London: Oxford University Press, 2009

Esolen, Anthony, *Out of the Ashes: Rebuilding American Culture*. Washington, D.C.: Regnery Gateway, 2022

——, *Defending Marriage: Twelve Arguments for Sanity*. Gastonia, NC: Saint Benedict Press, 2014

Fiedrowicz, Michael, *The Traditional Mass: History, Form, and Theology of the Classical Roman Rite*. Brooklyn, NY: Angelico Press, 2020

Gregory, Brad S., *The Unintended Reformation: How a Religious Revolution Secularized Society*. Cambridge, MA: Belknap Press, 2015

Horvat, John II, *Return to Order: From a Frenzied Economy to an Organic Christian Society*. York, PA: York Press, 2013

Jones, Andrew Willard, *The Two Cities: A History of Christian Politics*. Steubenville, OH: Emmaus Road Publishing, 2021

——, *Before Church and State: A Study of Social Order in the Sacramental Kingdom of St. Louis IX*. Steubenville, OH: Emmaus Road Publishing, 2017

Pernoud, Regine, *Those Terrible Middle Ages: Debunking the Myths*. San Francisco, CA: Ignatius Press, 2000

Pieper, Josef, *Leisure: the Basis of Culture*. San Francisco, CA: Ignatius Press, 2009

Storck, Thomas, *Foundations of a Catholic Political Order*. Waterloo, ON: Arouca Press, 2022

——, *An Economics of Justice and Charity: Catholic Social Teaching, Its Development and Contemporary Relevance*. Kettering, OH: Angelico Press, 2017

Waldstein, Edmund (Editor), *Integralism and the Common Good: Selected Essays from* The Josias (2 Vols.). Brooklyn, NY: Angelico Press, 2021–2022

Wiker, Benjamin and Hahn, Scott, *Politicizing the Bible: The Roots of Historical Criticism and the Secularization of Scripture 1300–1700*. New York: The Crossroad Publishing Company, 2013

——, *In Defense of Nature: The Catholic Unity of Environmental, Economic, and Moral Ecology*. Steubenville, OH: Emmaus Road Publishing, 2017

ABOUT THE AUTHOR

FR. JOSEPH LEVINE grew up in a liberal secular family and converted to the Catholic faith when he was 20 years old, after floundering for a couple of years at UC Berkeley. Then after spending four years in the US Coast Guard, he returned to school and graduated from Thomas Aquinas College in Santa Paula, California. He then embarked on what turned out to be a long and circuitous route to the priesthood passing through Portugal, Brazil, France, and three dioceses in the United States. He spent seven years with Canons Regular of the Holy Cross in Portugal and Brazil. He returned to the United States and became involved in the Society of St. John in Shohola, Pennsylvania. During that period he was ordained to the transitional diaconate at the Abbey of Notre Dame de Fontgombault in France. The Society of St. John was rich in its celebration of the traditional liturgy, but over the course of time grave problems emerged in the community, which led to his departure. After leaving the Society of St. John he attended St. Charles Borromeo Seminary under the auspices of the Diocese of Scranton. He then passed over to the Diocese of Paterson, before he was finally received and ordained by Bishop Robert Vasa, then Bishop of Baker, Oregon. As a priest he has served at St. Francis of Assisi parish in Bend, Blessed Sacrament in Ontario, Oregon, St. Bernard's in Jordan Valley, St. Peter's in The Dalles, and is currently Pastor at Holy Family in Burns, Oregon, where he drives 180 miles each weekend to serve three missions in the ranch country of Harney and Malheur Counties. He has become a regular speaker at the annual Sacred Liturgy Conference in the Pacific Northwest.